Restoring Antique Furniture

Restoring Antique Furniture

LESLIE WENN

with an historical introduction by
Martin Drury, the National Trust

Watson-Guptill Publications
New York

To my wife, Marjorie.

First published in the United States in
1975, second printing 1976, by
Watson-Guptill Publications,
a division of Billboard Publications, Inc.,
1515 Broadway, New York, New York 10036

Manufactured in Great Britain

Library of Congress Cataloging in
Publication Data
Wenn, Leslie.
Restoring antique furniture.

Includes index.

1. Furniture—Repairing. I. Title.
TT199.W46   1975   684.1'044   75-454?

ISBN 0-8230-4546-3

Designed by Chris Pocklington

Contents

Acknowledgements

I have been helped and encouraged by many people to write this book, and I am grateful to all concerned. I would like in particular to thank Miss Victoria Pelham-Burn, my first and most outstanding woman student whose devotion and patience with her work have inspired me to record my knowledge of restoration work; she has also given up much of her spare time to help me write this book.

I am also grateful to Mr John Lowe, the Principal, and Mr John Eves, the Director, of West Dean College (The Edward James Foundation) for giving me such ideal conditions in which to live and work on the first professional restoration course for antique furniture, where I am privileged to be the tutor. My appreciation also goes to Mr M. Trevor Venis, Chairman of the Cultural and Educational Trust of the British Antique Dealers' Association, for his part in promoting this course.

Leslie Wenn
West Dean, June 1974

Foreword

It gives me a great deal of pleasure to write the foreword to Leslie Wenn's excellent book, which sets out in clear language a lifetime of knowledge and experience so much needed today.

The question of proper restoration of antique furniture has been an abiding interest of mine for many years, because, unhappily, so many antiques were and still are being ruined by incompetent work. Also, many of the old skills in conservation and restoration have been in risk of dying out, much to the detriment of our national heritage and our country's position as the leading art and antique market of the world.

Some years ago the British Antique Dealers' Association in conjunction with West Dean College (The Edward James Foundation), set up the first course in conservation and restoration of antique furniture, to try to keep the old skills alive, and to train craftsmen for the future. At the start of the project we had to find the right tutor; somebody obviously with great skill, the ability to impart his knowledge and the willingness to put aside his own affairs and come to West Dean—a rare bird indeed! Here we owe to Leslie Wenn a great deal of gratitude, for, when I first asked him to join us, he had just retired and was busy restoring his own home and also relaxing a little after fifty years of hard work. Nevertheless, his sense of duty to our Association, of which he has been a member for many years, and his enthusiasm for the proposed course was such that he agreed to join us and at once showed himself to be a natural and gifted teacher. Highly skilled himself, he was able with charm and in an uncomplicated way to pass on his knowledge. As a result, many past students are now happily employed and doing work in the correct manner.

Leslie Wenn's book is particularly valuable because it teaches respect for our old furniture, which is what the art of furniture restoration is mainly about; and I feel sure that enthusiastic restorers will benefit greatly by reading it.

M. Trevor Venis
Chairman of the Cultural and Educational Committee
of the British Antique Dealers' Association

Introduction

There is a bewildering choice of books on antique furniture available to the student today. There are books on furniture history, specialist books on types and periods, collectors' guides, price guides, dictionaries and encyclopaedias. Very few are concerned with the care of furniture and with its restoration, and it is hoped that this book will help to fill the gap. It sets down in straight-forward language the knowledge and skills acquired by the author during more than fifty years' experience.

These very words draw attention to the limitations of such a book, for the written word could never claim to be a substitute for years spent at the bench. It was for a good reason that in more demanding times an aspiring cabinet-maker served an apprenticeship of seven years and this alone did not, of course, make him a good craftsman. Experience and a natural deftness are of equal importance. Nevertheless, the great majority of repairs that confront the restorer are a matter of following instructions. This book supplies those instructions, as well as a great many professional tips. Day by day the number of experienced craftsmen is becoming fewer and their time, in consequence more expensive. The wise collector, like the wise motor-car owner, will want to appreciate how to carry out running repairs and, in so doing, he will know a familiarity with the principles of craftsmanship that is denied to the furniture historian, who has never so intimately handled the objects of his study.

Both the collector and the restorer of antique furniture are recent phenomena. They replaced the patron and the cabinet-maker in the decade that preceded the First War. The great new houses of Victorian England were not furnished with antiques. New pieces were ordered from the leading makers of the day. No particular cachet attached to the possession of a set of eighteenth century chairs; a modern set of reproductions tended to be sturdier and looked much the same. Early oak furniture was collected by those with an antiquarian bent, in the belief that it was mediaeval (as early as 1761 Horace Walpole was urging his friends to look out for turned sixteenth century chairs, which could be had from farm-houses in Cheshire for three and sixpence), and French eighteenth century furniture, so much of which found its way into English ownership after the Revolution, was greatly prized. But the English equivalent though valued along with family portraits and an old house, as indications of respectable ancestry, was rarely collected for its own sake. Indeed, it would have been difficult for it to have been so, for the nineteenth century was, in the main, a period of great stability and the contents of old houses were not often dispersed.

By the 1890's this attitude had begun to change. The writings of Ruskin and Morris had awakened a new interest in all forms of craftsmanship and, in particular, that of England's recent past. In 1877 The Society for the Protection of Ancient Buildings had been founded; in 1895 followed the National Trust and by the end of the century many of the antique dealers, whose names are familiar today, were supplying the demands of a swiftly increasing number of collectors from premises in Bond Street, Oxford Street and the Tottenham Court Road. Even so, as late as 1909 the large workshop of one well-known dealer was still principally engaged in copying seventeenth and eighteenth century models.

The nineteen-twenties were for the collector a golden era. In the aftermath of the First War Victorian and Edwardian taste fell suddenly from favour and the craftsmanship of preceding centuries rose in the scales of general estimation. Innumerable country houses were sold up and their contents dispersed. Antique shops and sale-rooms abounded with four-poster beds, chests, oak chairs and panelling, as the old posting inns were modernised to accord with the image of the new motoring age. In this decade the foundations of some of the finest collections of English furniture in England and America were laid and the first informed books on the subject written. Among collectors there was often more enthusiasm than knowledge and the faker thrived. So plentiful was the supply of old furniture that a simple piece might not find a buyer unless it was embellished. Many an oak chest of drawers was veneered in walnut to this end and gateleg tables, mahogany urn stands and plain oak chests, to name a few of the most frequently 'improved' pieces, lost much of their interest and value to us today by the addition of carved detail.

As the number of collectors increased, so did the demand for craftsmen, who specialised in restoration. Many of those men, amongst them the author of this book, who have spent their lives rescuing antique furniture from decay, began their careers during these years. A new and rare combination of talents was required in

10

the restorer. To be a good craftsman was not enough. A knowledge of the history of styles and of the use of woods, an antiquarian's eye for the enhancing effects of time and wear were not demanded of the men in Chippendale's workshop, but are vital to successful restoration. It is fortunate that during the past fifty years there have been many men at work, in whom all these talents combined and that, whatever may happen in the future, the life of so much antique furniture has been indefinitely prolonged.

Often it is not only the ravages of time, rough handling and the furniture beetle that confront the restorer. Many pieces that come out of old houses have suffered from running repairs by the estate handyman or the local joiner. Other fine pieces, temporarily out of favour, have been adapted to perform some humble function, for which they were never designed. Some years ago an enterprising antique dealer came upon a Queen Anne double-arched walnut bureau-bookcase in the estate office of a house in Bedfordshire. Its finely figured veneers were obscured by a thick layer of dust and the greasy deposit left by oil lamps; bandings and mouldings had dried out, split and broken away. Its fall-front was secured by the type of long hinge that is used on out-house doors. Its pigeon holes and the small interior drawers were inscribed in ink by an eighteenth century hand with the names of different seeds, such as 'turnip' and 'parsnip', written with the archaic 's'. The silvering of its shaped and bevelled looking-glass plates had perished from the effects of damp, but although begrimed, they were intact and original to the piece with, a rare feature, stars cut into their arched tops. Victorian kitchen knobs had replaced the original brass handles. Long ago this dignified piece of furniture had been displaced and banished from the library or drawing room in which it had once stood. It had proved useful as an office desk and, though much degraded, had for this reason happily survived. Its restoration took two skilled restorers, cabinet-maker and polisher, more than a year and today it proudly represents its period in a fine collection of English furniture in America.

Every furniture historian, restorer and dealer has many such stories to tell, but I may, perhaps, be forgiven for recounting one other. An authority on eighteenth century cabinet-makers was asked to go through the many bills and inventories that happened to have been preserved in an 18th century house in Warwickshire. It was hoped to identify pieces described on the bills with those still in the house. As it turned out this proved to be possible in most of the main rooms, but there was one notable exception. A pair of gilt-wood marble-topped side-tables supplied in the 18th century at great expense by a local maker could nowhere be found. It was assumed that they had been given away or sold with, most uncharacteristically for the family in question, no record of the disposal kept among their papers. The following day the visitor went to church and there found one of the missing tables serving as the altar. In due course its pair was run to earth in the laundry, where, with no trace of its gilding remaining, cut down and a wooden top crudely nailed to it, it had served, perhaps for a century, as an ironing-board. Both tables were sent to London for repair and now, regilded and with new marble tops, they stand once again in the positions for which they were made.

These two stories happen to concern relatively important and valuable pieces of furniture, but there are many more humble pieces lying abandoned in garages and attics, which, with the aid of this book could be repaired and polished up and brought back into use. Many pieces of Victorian furniture, until recently long out of fashion, have been put away with a broken leg or threadbare upholstery and await a sympathetic restorer. With a knowledge of the basic principles of restoration it is often possible to pick up bargains in antique shops. With the present cost and scarcity of the professional restorer's time, restoring a damaged piece may not be an economic proposition for the dealer, but may, nonetheless, be an interesting and rewarding challenge to the amateur with free time and patience at his disposal.

It would give a false impression if these introductory paragraphs were to say nothing of the regrettable amount of bad restoration work from which antique furniture has always suffered. It was to a great extent the desire to prevent what he calls 'botched work' in the future that inspired the author to embark on the present book. By stressing the importance of his 'Golden Rules' of restoration and constantly drawing attention to the need for careful observation and exercise of the sense of touch, he encourages sensitivity in the restorer to the effects of age and emphasises the desirability of preserving as much original material as possible. These points are quite as important in restoration as technical knowledge and skill. There are many fine looking pieces to be seen in the London antique shops, which, through brutal over-restoration, are of little interest to the collector, who prefers his furniture to carry without shame the marks of honest old age. It is sometimes hard to restrain a craftsman, through genuine pride in his skill, from repainting, regilding or recarving, when a careful job of reviving, cleaning or refixing would be more appropraite. This tendency demonstrates again the difference between a good craftsman and a good restorer.

Work slowly, observing and feeling the effect of every cut of the chisel, every dab of the 'rubber' or stroke of the brush. This is, perhaps, the most important of all the valuable lessons of this book. And there is also one danger, of which the beginner should be warned. Most restoration work, as has been noted earlier, is a matter of following instructions, that is to say, technique, and, of course, technique will improve with experience. The restoration of oriental lacquer work, however, and the European imitation of it, usually known as 'japanning', is a field of restoration, into which the beginner should step with the greatest caution. Lacquered furniture, particularly red japanned furniture, in the seventeenth and eighteenth centuries was prized above all other, and today, due to its vulnerability to damage by furniture beetle and extremes of humidity, it is very rare. Many of the pieces that do survive have lost much of their value through inexperienced or excessive restoration. Small areas of damage can be dealt with by the beginner with the aid of the chapter dealing with the subject in this book, but usually, where lacquer is in bad condition, all its surfaces will be affected and repair to a small area will lead to disturbance of adjacent areas, and what seems to be a slight problem will escalate alarmingly. Such repairs require the attention, or at least advice of a specialist. Oriental lacquer, of which a great quantity was imported from China in the last century, is much more resilient and, so long as the restorer is deft with a brush and can copy faithfully, need not be approached with such wariness, but if at all in doubt it would be wise to consult an expert.

The earliest furniture that the restorer is likely to have on his bench are the oak pieces of the early seventeenth century. Mediaeval domestic furniture is very rare and what does survive is for the most part of an extremely rudimentary nature, the skills of the carver being devoted primarily to the embellishment of the furniture and fittings of ecclesiastical buildings. The furnishings of a mediaeval house comprised beds, benches, stools, trestle tables, livery cupboards for the storage of food and chests for the storage and transport of clothes, hangings and valuables. Only the last two were likely to be decorated with carving; the rest were unadorned and, when in use would be covered or hung with expensive textiles, to which far more importance was attached. The increasing prosperity of the sixteenth century and the greater emphasis on domestic permanence and comfort are apparent in both the variety of furniture that it produced and in the heavy carving, bulbous turning and elaborate inlay with which the great beds, court cupboards, side tables, long dining tables, arm chairs, chests, stools and cabinets were embellished. But, like that of earlier periods, Tudor and Elizabethan furniture is now rarely seen outside museums and the London salerooms.

Mercifully, however, pieces dating from the early seventeenth century are less scarce and the great boom in the furniture-making trade that followed the Restoration of Charles II in 1660 has ensured that furniture made during the last four decades of the century is still to be seen in antique shops all over England. Types of furniture common between 1620 and 1660 (see pages 18-21) were the chest, of both 'board' and panelled construction, the joined (or joint) stool, the armchair, small side tables, and presses. The last were high-waisted two- or three-tier cupboards with the upper or middle tier usually recessed behind the bulbous free-standing columns, the whole piece sometimes reaching massive proportions. Also made at this time were small hanging cupboards with pierced panels or panels composed of rows of spindle-turnings for the ventilated storage of food, and shallow portable boxes intended to contain books, documents or small articles of clothing. Many of the latter had sloping tops to provide a convenient surface for writing or reading.

The principal wood used during this period for all furniture and for much cottage and farm house furniture until well into the nineteenth century, was native oak. The durability of this timber has ensured its survival and its appeal today derives largely from the patina of age. Signs of heavy and, to us irresponsible, wear form part of this patina and care should be taken to preserve all bruises, chips, gouges and worn edges. They are honourable scars and the admirer of oak furniture prefers them to be seen and simply wax polished.

Not all 17th century furniture, however, was made of oak. The most common type of chair, for example, was that which is sometimes called the farthingale, or misleadingly, the Cromwellian chair, that is to say, an armless chair with a square seat, low back and four stretchers usually placed near the ground. Known in their day as Turkey chairs from the woollen material with which they were usually covered, they tended to be made of softwood and when their covering perished would be discarded and destroyed. A few were made of oak and it is these and those covered in leather that have survived.

Until 1660 the most common form of decoration comprised shallow carving on the forward-facing surfaces. Communications were poor in the seventeenth century and local differences of technique, particularly in carved ornament, were very pronounced. For the same reason change came slowly to remote parts of the country and furniture in the seventeenth century manner continued to be made well into the eighteenth, often making dating difficult.

The restoration of Charles II brought a sudden and conspicuous change in the development of English furniture. The native styles, which had evolved over two centuries, were overwhelmed by a flood of foreign ideas and techniques. From twenty years of exile on the continent the Court returned with a taste for luxury and sophistication that could only be suited by immigrant craftsmen from France and Holland. In the Great Fire of 1666 many thousands of houses were destroyed and the demand for furniture to fill those that replaced them brought about an enormous increase in the number of craftsmen at work in the city. Construction became lighter and more elegant; walnut displaced oak as the wood most favoured for the best pieces and the new techniques of marquetry and veneering superseded carving for the embellishment of flat surfaces. Chairs were now lightly constructed of polished walnut or japanned beech. Their backs became higher, their seats smaller. At first they were caned (in imitation of Dutch and French chairs) and backs, legs and stretchers were elaborately carved, the seat made comfortable by a squab cushion. Later the proportions became yet more attenuated,

14

carved decoration more sparing and seat and back caned or upholstered in cut velvet or some other imported silk fabric. Families no
longer dined in the hall with their servants, but withdrew to the
privacy of smaller rooms, where gateleg tables of oak, or, more
rarely, of walnut were set up and covered with cloths. Great ad-
vances were made in the manufacture of plate glass. It remained
expensive, but large sheets were now in production. They were
silvered behind and either mounted in 'cushion' frames with arched
fretwork crestings, or encased in embossed silver or set in carved
gilt-wood frames in the French manner.

The free standing secretaire arrived from Holland in the 1670's. At
first it was a straight-topped cabinet with a vertical fall-front and
mounted on an open stand of turned legs joined by stretchers. Later
the writing cabinet was given a sloping fall-front and ingeniously
combined with a bookcase and a chest of drawers (see page 25). The
top might be arched or double arched and surmounted by gilded
finials. By the end of the century the familiar small fall-front bureau
with drawers below and no bookcase above was being made in
increasing numbers.

The extreme richness of the seventeenth century interior, composed of expensive silks and velvets, marquetry, figured walnut,
looking-glass, silver, heavily moulded wainscotting in tall narrow
panels and furniture of exaggerated outline, was greatly enhanced by
lacquer cabinets and by immense Coromandel screens imported
from the Orient. The former would be mounted on carved gilded or
silvered stands made in England and sometimes surmounted by
matching crestings. So popular were these cabinets that they were
made in great numbers by European craftsmen, either from the
panels of imported screens or in oak veneered in pearwood, coated
with gesso and painted and varnished in a not very convincing
pastiche of oriental work. This process, known as japanning, could
employ a black ground or, less often, blue, green, red or ivory.
Chairs, bureaux, card tables, chests of drawers, torchères and the
interiors of entire rooms were treated in this way and the fashion
persisted well into the eighteenth century.

The eighteenth century saw a return to simpler, and more practical designs. Marquetry and the turned leg gave way to figured
veneers and the cabriole. Furniture was in the main smaller and
more robust. Chairs had lower backs; were more compact and more
rounded in outline; back splats and seat rails had broad flat surfaces
to show off the figure of the walnut to good effect. The stretcher
disappeared, the drop-in seat was introduced and, though these
tended to be covered in needlework, less importance was now attached to the use of textiles, and carving was often reduced to no
more than a simple shell on the knee or seat rail. Chests of drawers,
bureaux and side-tables all responded to a demand for neat compact
furniture, simply cross- or feather-banded and faced with veneers
carefully chosen for the beauty of their figure. Among large pieces

were the tall-boy, the chest of drawers mounted on a stand, and the bureau bookcase. The two former finally superseded the lift-top chest and (temporarily) the press for the storage of clothes. Expensive tastes were catered for by side tables, pairs of torchères and pier glasses, coated in gesso, carved in shallow relief and laid with gold or silver leaf. With the increasing emphasis on domesticity and entertaining on a small scale, card games enjoyed an unprecedented popularity and tables designed specifically for the purpose, rare in the seventeenth century, were made in large numbers during the reign of Queen Anne. They were of walnut or japan with fold-over tops lined with velvet and were sometimes equipped with veneered recesses for counters and circular rimmed platforms for candlesticks. Japanning also remained fashionable for chairs, bureaux, chests of drawers and torchères.

The fashion for smooth lines and the minimum of carving did not last long. The squat silhouette, ponderous proportions and heavy carving of chairs made during the 1720's and 30's were closer in feeling to the oak furniture of eighty years before than anything that had enjoyed popularity since. The claw and ball foot replaced the simple pad and the plain rounded 'shepherd's crook' arm was extended and carved in the form of eagles' heads.

Cabinet furniture became massive and architectural. By the 1730's dense, dark mahogany was being imported from San Domingo. This wood was hard and strong; its hardness enabled the carver to achieve decorative detail of great crispness and precision; its strength made possible the fretted galleries and finely pierced splats that are characteristic of mid-eighteenth century furniture. Mahogany was cut from giant tropical trees and large table tops were formed of single solid planks. Later in the century the paler Cuban mahogany was preferred for its wider grain and varied figure ('fiddle-back', 'plum-pudding' and 'curl'). Where mahogany from San Domingo (sometimes called 'Spanish') had been used for the most part in the solid, Cuban was more often sliced and veneered on an oak carcase. The many pattern-books published during the middle decades of the century, of which Thomas Chippendale's *Gentleman & Cabinet-Maker's Director* of 1754 is only the most famous, take full advantage of the known qualities of this versatile wood and recommend a series of Gothic, Rococo, 'Chinese' and French curvilinear designs that could not have been achieved with any native European timber.

It is perhaps, not too broad a generalisation to say that it was the archaeologist who presided over furniture, as over all branches of the decorative arts, during the last four decades of the eighteenth century and the first two of the nineteenth. The excavation of the Roman cities of Herculaneum and Pompeii stirred the imagination of the civilised world and, through the pattern books of architects and designers, the decorative devices employed by the Romans to embellish their buildings and sculpture – the anthemion, the patera, the Vitruvian scroll, the acanthus, the urn and the husk – all found

16

their way into the repertory of the English cabinet-maker. Rome provided the detail for chairs that were lighter, smaller and more elegant than ever before with oval, heart- or shield-shaped backs, for half-round card- and side-tables on square, tapering legs ending in spade feet, for gilded oval looking-glasses, surmounted by urns from which cascaded delicate strings of husks, for glazed cabinets, book-cases and secretaires with thin astragals describing intricate patterns, for small *bonheur-du-jours,* or lady's writing tables. Satinwood was used from the 1780's usually as a veneer and less often in the solid for chairs. Cheap and attractive furniture was made in pine or beech, painted and decorated with sparing neo-classical motifs. In general, at the end of the eighteenth century furniture reached an extreme of elegance and refinement that was often at the expense of structural soundness.

This criticism could not be made of the furniture of the last period that falls within the scope of this book. After 1800 furniture became increasingly massive and sturdy. Rosewood was most frequently used for veneers as well as the exotic striped calamander, often in con-junction with gilt-bronze mounts and inlaid with lines of brass. Ancient Greece was the inspiration of the period and the *klismos,* the sabre-legged chair with the square, raked back, depicted in ancient sculpture, provided the model for the Regency chair. The sofa-table and the Davenport were innovations, as was the circular centre-table on a single turned stem. Much furniture was painted and gilded and the colour chosen was often green, in an attempt to simulate bronze. A further significant innovation was the extending dining table on two or more pillars, each ending in four splayed legs with brass shoes and castors. Tables with additional leaves that could be inserted between the supported sections had been known in the 18th century, but it now achieved its most practical form and finally superseded the old arrangement of a number of small tables that would be set up for each meal.

This brief and, inevitably sketchy, survey of the course of English furniture over more than two centuries will have given the aspiring restorer some idea of the great variety of the tasks that will confront him; in the pages that follow the author will equip him to meet them with confidence, and embark on a totally absorbing pastime, which, as a source of relaxation and satisfaction, is second only to that of creation itself.

Oak chest, the front
formed by one board.
Early seventeenth century.
Leonard Lassalle

Oak chest, the front, top
and sides panelled, the
frame secured by mortice
and tenon joints. c.1660.
Leonard Lassalle

Following Page
Oak armchair, the back
panelled, the front legs
and arm uprights turned
out of single pieces of
timber. c.1660. *Leonard
Lassalle*

18

19

Opposite Page

Oak 'joined' or 'joint' stool, on turned splayed legs. Mid seventeenth century. This was the commonest form of seat furniture until the very end of the seventeenth century, when the chair came into more general use and ceased to be reserved for those of high rank. *Leonard Lassalle*

Oak side table, on turned legs joined by turned plain stretchers. Mid seventeenth century. *Leonard Lassalle*

Oak gateleg table on turned legs, the drop-leaves supported on retractable frames, cut and shaped out of oak planks. c.1670. *Leonard Lassalle*

This Page

Oak side chair on turned legs, the front legs joined by a turned stretcher, the back legs carved in shallow relief, the upper rail depicting a stylised male head. c.1660. This type of chair, local to Yorkshire and Derbyshire, continued to be made with many slight variations well into the eighteenth century. *Leonard Lassalle*

Oak dresser on shaped supports. c.1680. The dresser, with many local variations, has continued to be made up to the present day. *Leonard Lassalle*

Black 'japanned' side chairs with caned back and seat. c.1690. More expensive chairs of this type were made of walnut and polished; this example is of beech. *Spink & Son Ltd.*

21

Small walnut bureau, on turned legs, the oak carcase veneered in burr walnut. c.1690. *Mallett & Son (Antiques) Ltd.*

Detail below

Walnut side chair, the back and seat rail veneered in burr walnut, the cabriole legs and shell motif carved in solid walnut. c.1725. *Mallett & Son (Antiques) Ltd.*

22

Walnut bureau, the oak carcase veneered in burr and straight-grain walnut, the drawer fronts cross- and feather-banded. c.1715. The handles and key escutcheons are not original. *Mallet & Son (Antiques) Ltd.*

Walnut chest of drawers, the oak carcase veneered in burr and straight-grain walnut, the drawer fronts cross- and feather-banded. c.1715. Note the brushing-slide, the surface of which, not seen in this photograph, is lined in green baize set in a broad cross-banding. This piece would have formed part of the furnishings of a bedroom. *Mallett & Son (Antiques) Ltd.*

23

Walnut and parcel-gilt wall mirror, the cresting veneered on a shaped pine board and the moulded surround to the glass carved from solid cross-grained walnut. c.1720. Such mirrors, often described in contemporary inventories as 'wall-sconces', were expensive items, owing to the high cost of making plate-glass. The candle arm is a later addition; the design allows for two separate candle arms. *Mallett & Son (Antiques) Ltd.*

Walnut side-table on cabriole legs ending in pointed pad feet, the top and drawer fronts cross- and feather-banded. c.1715. *Spink & Son Ltd.*

24

Red 'japanned' bureau cabinet with 'chinoiseries' in gold and black, painted on a vermilion ground. c.1710. The pine carcase is veneered in pear-wood (chosen for its lack of pronounced grain), coated with gesso and painted in imitation of oriental lacquerwork. Note the dark tone of the interior, which has been less exposed to the light, and the retractable candle-slides, so placed that the light would be reflected in the mirror-glass doors. The bracket feet are not original and have been replaced bun feet. Red 'japanned' furniture has always been much prized and a great deal was exported in the eighteenth century, particularly to Spain and Portugal. *Mallett & Son (Antiques) Ltd.*

Detail shown overleaf

Mahogany side chair c.1760. This design is based on those in Chippendale's *The Gentleman & Cabinet-Maker's Director (1754 & 1762)*. The lower part of the frame is quite plain, denoting a comparatively inexpensive chair. *Mallett & Son (Antiques) Ltd.*

Mahogany kettle or urn stand. c.1765. Note the crisp carving, to which mahogany is especially well suited, and the slight bow in the top. Solid timber, cut thin, tends to warp in this way. *Mallett & Son (Antiques) Ltd.*

Mahogany chest of drawers. c.1765. This piece exploits the qualities of mahogany as does the walnut chest shown on p.23. *Mallett & Son (Antiques) Ltd.*

Following page
Mahogany kettle or urn stand, with fret-cut gallery. c.1765. This was more stable than the previous example and provided a slide, on which to rest the tea cup. *Mallett & Son (Antiques) Ltd.*

Carved giltwood mirror. c.1765. The naturalistic rococo detail is typical of the liveliness of mid-eighteenth century designs inspired by the pattern books of Chippendale and Thomas Johnson amongst other designers. *Christies*

Mahogany tea-caddy. c.1760. The centre compartment contains a glass bowl, in which the tea was blended. Tea itself was stored in the flanking containers of wood lined with tinfoil.

28

Mahogany shield-back armchair. c.1775. Late eighteenth century chairs became increasingly light in appearance and frail in construction. The stretcher was almost invariably omitted. *Christies*

Marquetry card table, the top and frieze veneered in 'fiddle-back' sycamore marquetry, the cabriole legs of solid mahogany. c.1775. *Mallett & Son (Antiques) Ltd.*

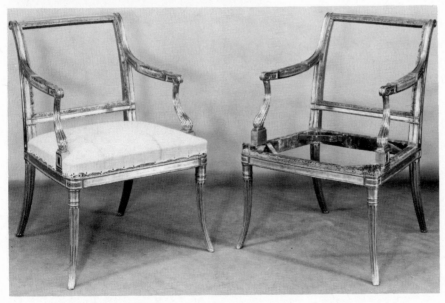

Pair of giltwood armchairs (partially upholstered). c.1800. This design, based on that of the ancient Greek *klismos,* occurs with many variations throughout the first three decades of the nineteenth century. The light construction of this chair indicates a date of around 1800. Note the exposed tacking rails around the seat and back and the strengthening struts, which became necessary when the stretcher was omitted. The frames are of beech, gessoed and gilded. *Mallett & Son (Antiques) Ltd.*

29

Pembroke table, veneered in satinwood, cross-banded in tulipwood with ebony stringing & painted decoration. c.1790. Painted decoration was a cheap alternative to marquetry and enjoyed brief popularity during the decades spanning the turn of eighteenth and nineteenth centuries. *Mallett & Son (Antiques) Ltd.*

One of a pair of painted candle-stands. c.1790. Painted furniture could be made of cheap timber (beech or pine) and was therefore an inexpensive alternative to furniture veneered in the more exotic woods. Being by nature more subject to attack by woodworm it is now rare. Original painted decoration should be carefully preserved and never over-painted. *Mallett & Son (Antiques) Ltd.*

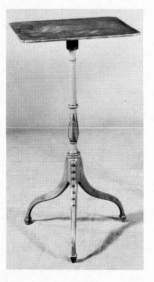

30

Detail of a painted card table of pine and beechwood, carved in imitation of bamboo and decorated with scenes in *chinoiserie*. This detail shows the type of damage that can be caused to painted furniture by central heating. Reduction in humidity causes the wood to shrink, thereby wrinkling the coating of gesso and paint, which then begins to flake off. *Mallett & Son (Antiques) Ltd.*

Mahogany sofa table. c.1805. The broad-long-grain banding is unusual, but the form with many variations was very popular from about 1800 to 1830. *Mallett & Son (Antiques) Ltd.*

Mahogany armchair with caned sides, back and seat. c.1810. Compare the weightiness of this chair with the pair of giltwood armchairs. Such chairs were frequently made for libraries between about 1800 and 1820. *Christies*

Rosewood worktable. c.1810. Rosewood veneer inlaid with brass was an innovation of the early nineteenth century. This lady's work-box has lost its pleated silk bag for storing silks and wools. *Mallett & Son (Antiques) Ltd.*

Detail of a Pembroke table, veneered in satinwood and sycamore, cross-banded in tulipwood and boxwood with ebony stringing and marquetry in holly and stained boxwood. c.1785. *Mallett & Son (Antiques) Ltd.*

31

Circular marquetry centre table veneered in burr walnut and rosewood with marquetry of various exotic woods. c.1860. As the nineteenth century progressed taste became increasingly flamboyant. This table is an example of the type of furniture displayed at the Great Exhibition of 1851 and made for about twenty years afterwards. *Christies*

Mahogany 'balloon' back chair. c.1870. Variations of this chair were made from 1850 until the end of the century. This is a particularly ponderous example. *Sotheby's Belgravia*

Small ormolu mounted writing table in the Louis XV style, cross-banded in kingwood, the top inset with a leather panel. Made by W. Woods, Queen Street, Southwark Bridge Road, London. c.1860. Throughout the nineteenth century Paris was the centre of the cultural world and French eighteenth century models were painstakingly copied by English makers. *Sotheby's Belgravia*

Burr walnut and marquetry glazed side cabinet. c.1860. This is a good example of the massive, richly decorated furniture that was produced in great quantities during the 1850s and '60s. *Sotheby's Belgravia*

33

Painted satinwood card table. c.1900. There was a vogue for painted satinwood furniture at the end of the century imitating that produced in the last decade of the eighteenth century. Much of it, like this table, is difficult to distinguish from the original. The full-blown roses and cartouche of fruit are clues to the true date. *Sotheby's Belgravia*

Oak armchair. c.1905. Reacting against the prevailing taste for furniture, which they regarded as decadent, a small group of makers devoted themselves from the 1880s to furniture that was beautiful because it was simple, unpretentious and utilitarian. This chair is an original design using traditional country materials. *Sotheby's Belgravia*

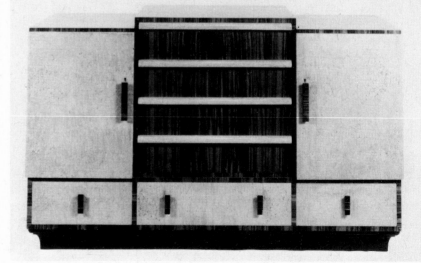

Pine and ebony cabinet for a bedroom, by Heal & Son, 1915.

34

CHAPTER ONE

Understanding Furniture

This book is concerned with the restoration of antique furniture, but before we embark on any restoration work we must understand quite a bit about antique furniture. It is largely lack of understanding that leads to the disastrous gash repairs one so often meets in the trade. Think of the great skills used in the construction of antique furniture, particularly in the eighteenth century, under conditions we could not tolerate today. Craftsmen then produced the most beautiful and accurate work in furniture ever known, so surely it is not asking too much of us to use all the knowledge and skill we can muster to restore some of these pieces that have suffered so much at the hands of local handymen or through sheer neglect.

HOW TO RECOGNIZE GOOD FURNITURE

Let us take eighteenth-century furniture first, as I feel it was our greatest period in furniture-making. You only need common sense to recognize a piece of quality. First stand back and look at the design, the way the piece is balanced. I have to talk in general terms, but as most pieces of furniture have a front and back, a top and bottom, and possibly doors and drawers, you will be able to apply this knowledge to your particular piece. If you watch the expert, he will, before doing anything else, stand and look at the piece because his first impressions can be important; then, if he has satisfied himself on the first impression, that the general design and balance are in order, he usually takes out a drawer and looks for the finely-cut dovetails and the accurate workmanship in construction of a well made drawer, the oxidized colour of the timber that has never been stained, but only mellowed with age. Should you be looking at a

Opposite Page

Rosewood and burr maple sideboard by Waring & Gillow. c.1925. This piece is typical of the best commercial furniture supplied by the big manufacturers during what is now known as the Art Deco period. It formed part of a dining-room 'suite'.

chair or small piece of furniture, it is worth turning the piece upside down; often you can see more of the construction and judge the quality of the piece from the underside than through the polished top surfaces.

The timber used can also tell you a lot: a good piece will be made from good quality timber which is usually very heavy and hard, whereas perhaps a country-made or poorer quality piece will be made of cheaper timber, be light to handle, and have an open, more porous grain of a more sappy nature. This is quite easily recognizable if one can compare the two. A lot of furniture is well made, but does not stand up to finer pieces for design and quality of timber; in the main these are country-made pieces and not produced by the leading makers in the towns. We must not ignore country-made furniture as some of it has great charm and beauty and is more often within the reach of the 'not so well-to-do' collector as far as price is concerned. Restoration should be treated with as much care as for the finer pieces of furniture. The colour of country furniture can be as attractive as the colour of the more expensive pieces and therefore must be handled with the same attention in restoration work and the reward will be as great.

I feel that a good piece of old furniture can almost become part of the family: it is something we live with and see every day, and the longer we live with it the more fond of it we become; it is a work of art that for many reasons will not be made again in this plastic age We cannot produce timber of the quality used in the past; in the eighteenth century one generation of cabinet-makers laid down the timber for the next generation to use, this timber was cut into planks, stacked correctly and allowed to dry out very slowly for perhaps fifty years, expanding and contracting as the atmospheric conditions changed until it finally reached the ideal dry state needed for furniture. That is why today one can find a dining-table leaf 2 ft. or more wide and $\frac{3}{4}$ in. thick – just one board, with no reinforcement of any kind, and yet as straight as the day it was made; it has not warped or twisted at all. This is due to the way the timber was seasoned in the first place and also the way it was selected for its purpose. We have overcome this problem today by using multi-ply woods and veneering for table tops. This is only one reason why these works of art will not be made in this day and age. We have too few craftsmen today who have all the necessary skills, and even if they have they cannot afford to use them because it would be too time-consuming for the market. So let's preserve what we have inherited from the masters of the past.

CHAPTER TWO

Behaviour of Wood
in Furniture

Every restorer should thoroughly understand wood. I always feel it
is a living thing because it is very seldom quite still. Even after a few
hundred years, movement still goes on in all woods. For instance, I
have seen genuine pieces of early eighteenth-century furniture suddenly develop big cracks, particularly in the ends and tops of pieces,
after central heating has been installed in the house. This is because
previously they were in conditions where the wood could expand
during the cool of the night and contract during the rise of
temperature in the daytime. In a sense the wood was breathing.
With central heating the wood is subjected to constant heat, so it
contracts and continues to shrink, the measurement across the grain
becomes less and less, and the board is getting narrower all the time.
In the carcase of a piece of furniture where the boards are invariably
secured in position, this shrinkage goes on until it reaches breaking
point and the board splits at its weakest point. If these conditions
continue the piece of furniture will eventually twist, warp and crack
to such a degree that even the skilled furniture-restorer would
despair. Fortunately humidifiers are now being introduced to help
counteract this state of affairs, and bowls of flowers and indoor
plants can help quite a bit to prevent very dry conditions.

As dryness brought about by heat will cause shrinkage, so
dampness makes the grain begin to expand. This will show itself
mostly where wide boards are used in furniture. This was allowed for
by cabinet-makers using solid woods (that is to say not veneered) by
using a narrow frame to support a large panel, the panel resting
freely in a groove. The panel was *not* glued into the groove and so
was allowed to expand and contract quite freely, thus avoiding a
split occurring in the middle of the board.

WARPING

Today multiple plywood is employed mainly for tops and large areas of boards in construction of furniture because this plywood is made up of veneers laid in opposite directions of grain so that it cannot split from shrinking in one direction, but unless secured by a very sound frame it can still warp and twist under the strain caused by this wood movement. I have seen iron plates let into card-table tops where the power of wood shrinkage has bent the iron. You cannot fight this great power by force, but much of the warp can be overcome by cunning. There are many approaches to this problem: bearing in mind what has caused the warp in any particular case and applying the reverse effect is one. If you take a piece of very thin wood, preferably as wide as possible (say the bottom of a matchbox which is often made of wood) and wet one side, it will immediately take up a bowed shape because one side is wet and one side is dry; wet the other side and it will begin to straighten again. This is because when you wetted one side it began to expand, forcing the wood to a curve or bow shape, and then having applied the same treatment to the other side you balanced the forces at work. This simple illustration can be helpful in overcoming a warped board.

In the case of a card table where you have a polished surface on the top side and baize lining on the under side you will often find the top flap does not close down flat. This is because one side of the board has been polished and the other side is practically raw wood except for the baize lining; therefore when the top flap is closed, very little heat is able to reach the baize side of the board, causing the board to bow slightly. This particularly applies to a card table which is little used. Much of this trouble can be corrected by leaving the top flap of the table open and resting against the wall, especially when the room is at a fairly high temperature. The wall helps to insulate the top side of the table and all the direct heat of the room goes on to the raw underside, making it dry. If a card table is opened up in this way from time to time much correction will take place and in many cases the table top will become quite flat again.

A good example of how to keep a board straight can be seen in many mid-eighteenth-century dining tables where loose leaves are inserted in order to increase the length of the table. These loose leaves are usually fairly wide boards and usually very straight, partly because carefully chosen well seasoned timber was used, but mainly because the leaves were polished on both sides of the board – not perhaps so much on the underside but enough to give the same insulation on the top as on the bottom; thus the wood did not change its shape and could go on expanding and contracting with the changes of temperature quite evenly.

IS IT AUTHENTIC?

Remembering this particular nature of wood is helpful to the expert when judging a piece of antique furniture for authenticity. If the piece is genuine, most of the outside surfaces will be slightly bowed and not flat as when they were made; this is because the piece has been subjected to room temperature during its life, and the inside, being unpolished wood, has dried out more over the course of time than the outside which has been protected by a coat of polish; so we have more shrinkage on the inside of the board, causing this slightly round contour outside.

This will particularly apply to furniture of the Queen Anne period where hardwood veneers, such as walnut, were laid on softwood, usually pine. The pine will dry out and shrink more quickly than hardwood and the veneers were often laid across the grain of the pine, thus putting up more resistance to shrinkage on the outside of the piece, and so encouraging the pine base to shrink. The result is very noticeable in early eighteenth-century furniture. I must remind you that there is, of course, very little shrinkage in the *length* of a piece of wood: all this movement comes in the width of the board. The expert uses this knowledge when looking at a round top of a table; he knows that if the piece is genuine it should measure considerably less across the grain than in the length of the wood. Although it was a true circle when it was made, the years have caused a natural shrinkage to take place, but only in the width of the grain. The result of this seasoning can be found all over a piece of original period furniture – in drawer bottoms and sides, in back-boards, and everywhere you care to look, to a major or minor degree, depending on the quality and construction of the piece.

COLOUR OF WOOD

Another interesting characteristic of wood is that the depth of colour increases with age. Although the colour of timber can vary according to its source of origin, this is nothing compared with the colour change through age. As an extreme example, compare the colour of a piece of twentieth-century oak with that of a piece of seventeenth-century oak: the former is just off-white, the latter a deep rich brown. This change too is very noticeable in eighteenth-century mahogany: from the beginning to the end of one century the colour can range from a pale warm brown to a deep rich brown. Some allowance must be made for the particular type of mahogany, but in the main it can be a very useful guide. But do not be deceived by the polished surface colour, because this may be faded from exposure to light over the years, producing perhaps a pale honey colour on a piece of very dark mahogany. This fading is in the wood itself but only to a minute degree, and often lost in the hands of a careless furniture-restorer.

I have referred only to wood that has been cut to show its true colour. This test, of course, can be of little use in detecting the authenticity of a piece of furniture, because the piece could have been made recently using old wood from other furniture, but it is important for the restorer when matching his wood for repair work.

Wood in general is a very versatile material: it can be jointed, bent, dyed and worked in many ways, it has colour and beauty of grain, and is a most pleasant medium to handle. There is no other material that matches it, particularly in furniture.

PESTS AND DISEASE

There are, however, such disadvantages as beetles, fungus, disease and dry rot, but we can cope with these. I will not go too deeply into this subject because there are chemical preparations to deal with each of these problems, and full instructions are on the packages sold for the purpose. Most common is the furniture beetle, whose offspring is the woodworm. Having treated the affected parts with worm-killer, we have the problem of making good the damage. It was common at one time to impregnate the worm area with hot size or very thin glue in order to help reinforce the part weakened by worm destruction; today one can buy resin solutions with chemical hardeners for injecting into the channels made by the woodworm so as to reinforce the weakened part. This way we can preserve more of the original and also make the wood strong enough to joint onto should any be missing. This process is very useful in making good bun feet or bracket feet, which often suffer through worm, and at one time would have had to be replaced; these can now be saved.

Replacing veneer on the foot of a walnut bureau
The Antique Collector

CHAPTER THREE

Equipping a Workshop

The restoration of antique furniture is a very large subject, but in general practice the same principles apply to all ages of furniture, although different techniques are used for furniture made of different woods and of different ages.

I must assume that the student has a keen interest in and some knowledge of old furniture, and it would also be to the student's advantage to have had some experience in woodwork and the handling of tools. But I shall take him from the beginning as far as tools are concerned because we are dealing with materials not common to woodworkers or metalworkers – that is to say old wood which has become hard and brittle with age, and yet which can be cut and shaped to perfection if the tools used are ground and sharpened to suit.

Before we take our first piece of furniture for restoration, we must establish our workshop. We need plenty of daylight and a reasonably good temperature of about 70°F. These two factors are essential because only in good daylight can we recognize the colour and age of the wood which is being replaced in the repair work, and in a warm shop the wood will be dry and the glue will harden more quickly. Also, on the finishing side of restoration, we will be using chemicals, and it is only at a temperature of about 70° that the chemical reaction we need takes place.

I strongly advise the use of the old-fashioned scotch glue (animal glue) on repair work, as this is the only glue used on all old furniture. Thus, in the case of re-gluing an old joint, the newly applied scotch glue will amalgamate with the traces of existing glue already in the original joint and make a perfect bond. The modern chemical glues may not do this, and the joint could possibly split again later.

In some cases the thickness of the solution could be enough to keep the two surfaces apart, bearing in mind that the original joinery was a wood-to-wood contact. The furniture was assembled dry before gluing was done, and when finally glued the thin animal glue that was used simply went into the pores of the grain and made a perfect seal. No thickness of glue was left in the joint, whether it was a mortice and tenon joint, a dovetail or the jointing of two boards together, and thus a perfect wood-to-wood contact was made. If one uses a thickness of glue to make a joint tight, the life of the joint would be as long as the life of the glue used. Most glues shrink or harden in time, when the glue shrinks the joint becomes loose and falls apart; when the glue becomes rock hard, it can split through vibration in use, and thus the joint gives way. I have gone over this ground because it is so important *not* to rely on the strength of the glue in repair work or in introducing a new part. If the student puts his faith in good joinery it will not fail him. The fine examples of old furniture we have in our possession today would not have survived had the old craftsmen relied on glue for strength.

As far as the workshop equipment is concerned, a **carpenter's bench** and a **vice** of almost any kind will do. There is one machine that is essential, and the student will understand why later. This is a small **circular saw.** It need not be an expensive item to start with, although one could perhaps go in for something more elaborate if working professionally. The next items we need are a range of **sash cramps** and **hand screws,** or **G cramps** as they are sometimes called. The sash cramps are mainly used for cramping up mortice and tenon joints and carcase work when re-glued. The hand screws are used mainly to hold down small pieces of wood and old pieces of veneer while the glue is drying. Other types of spring clips and masking tape can also serve to hold pieces of old veneer and beading in position while the glue is drying.

Although a full kit of cabinet-making tools is essential professionally, for the beginner a few tools only are needed to start with, and I would suggest the following, in addition to those already mentioned:

    One small panel saw

    One dovetail saw

    One hand fret-saw

    Chisels: $\frac{1}{8}''$, $\frac{1}{4}''$, $\frac{1}{2}''$, $\frac{3}{4}''$, and a few small gouges as a minimum

    Carpenter's brace, and bits: $\frac{3}{8}''$, $\frac{1}{2}''$, $\frac{3}{4}''$, $1''$, as a minimum

    Screwdrivers and bradawl

    Wheel brace and bits

    One steel plane, 6″ or 7″

    One bull-nosed plane, 3″ or 4″

    One thin cabinet-maker's steel scraper (a very essential tool)

    One small pin hammer (suitable for driving in fine veneer pins)

One larger hammer
One coarse and one fine oil-stone for sharpening
A small bench-type motorized grinding wheel
One glue pot (2 chamber type)
Rule
Square
Scribe-marker

For the more advanced student, a **woodturning lathe** becomes a useful tool as turned woodwork appears quite often in antique furniture. Legs, rails, patries, etc. have to be replaced sometimes or a damaged part of a turned column may have to be replaced, and of course without a lathe this type of repair would be quite impossible. I will not attempt to teach you how to use a lathe as there are books on this subject, but once you are familiar with woodcutting tools a little experience and good common sense can see you through.

With this skeleton tool kit, most restoration work on the woodwork side can be done. Expensive tools are not the most important thing, although no doubt very helpful. I have seen some people do extremely fine work with a penknife; on the other hand, I have known people with the finest possible collection of tools get nowhere in craftsmanship. It is the person behind the tool that matters. I use the word person and not man because I have met some women whom I consider to be in the top class. Women in many cases have a better sense of touch than men, and a sense of touch is very important in shaping wood, and also in assessing the correct level of flushness of a piece of old veneer that has been put in, or other damages that have been put right. The tips of the fingers can tell one more than the eye can in many cases.

For cutting in small pieces of veneer, a $\frac{3}{4}''$ **chisel** is, I think, a handy size, but first it needs to be ground to a fairly long bevel (see figure I), then sharpened on an oil-stone so that we have an almost razor-like edge. Now we come to our **circular saw:** we need this for cutting a thin piece of veneer from an old piece of furniture of about the same date and colour. In the case of a Victorian chest, there should be no difficulty at all in finding a piece of Victorian mahogany. If it is an eighteenth-century chest of drawers, then you will have to watch your local sale rooms or junk stalls for some mahogany of a similar period.

All shaping should be done with **planes, chisels** and **scrapers,** using **abrasive papers** only for the final finishing. Coarse abrasives are only suitable for woodwork that is to be painted, as the scratches then make a key for the paint. But you cannot have any scratches in wood which is to be finished with a polished surface showing the beauty of the wood grain, as in old furniture.

It is important to remember that the modern methods of sanding machines and spray finishes with artificial wood-filler may give superb finishes on modern furniture, but if applied to antiques would be disastrous.

A **cabinet-maker's scraper** is essential – just a piece of flexible steel plate, and yet if sharpened properly and used correctly it can do a job that no other tool can (see figure 1). Scrapers are made in various thicknesses: the very finest are made for skimming the top off a heavily lacquered or varnished surface (for instance, one can cut off the orange peel effect cause by a spray gun finish and leave a fine flat surface ready for final polishing). But we are more concerned with a rather thicker, less flexible scraper which can take off a very thin shaving from wood.

SHARPENING

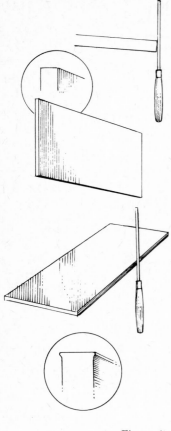

The method of sharpening is quite simple, but takes a bit of practice to get the best results. First we have to produce a perfectly square edge on the two long sides of the scraper. This is done by filing the edge absolutely flat and then grinding down on an oil-stone to remove any file marks that may be left, so that we finish up with a perfectly sharp square edge, with no roughness or burrs but a fine polished finish. The reason is that this fine edge is to be turned over to form a tiny cutting blade. This is done by drawing a piece of smooth hardened steel under strong pressure right along this edge, as shown in figure 1. I prefer to use a good old wood chisel for the purpose because the end is always polished from the sharpening stone and the steel is hard enough to overcome the softer metal of the scraper, although many cabinet-makers use a marking awl as the rounded surface of the awl makes it easier to push on the burr or cutting edge of the scraper. To get the best edge on the scraper, lay your scraper flat on the bench and hold it down with your left hand; then, pressing hard against the edge of the scraper with your awl or chisel, and at an angle slightly off the square of your previously finished edge, draw sharply and firmly along this edge; this will establish the tiny cutting edge shown in the illustration. If you do not make sufficient burr with one stroke of the awl, another stroke can be made, but a smoother and more retaining edge is obtained if done in one stroke.

Figure 1

To use a scraper to best advantage you need both hands because you get the perfect cut when the scraper is slightly bent. Hold each end of the scraper with your fingers pressing on the front and your

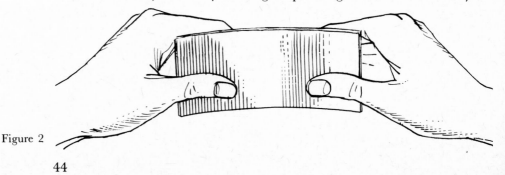

Figure 2

44

thumbs pressing in the middle of the scraper from behind, making the scraper bow slightly; thus the corners of the tool cannot stick into the wood, but the major part of the blade is in contact with what you are cutting (figure 2). You will find that by changing the angle at which you hold your scraper you can increase or decrease the amount of cut you make. You will soon find the best angle for holding for maximum cut and this should be the same angle that you held your awl when putting on this burr cutting edge. This tool may take quite a time to get used to, but it is necessary to master it.

GRINDING AND SHARPENING TOOLS

It is very important that you grind and sharpen your own tools, particularly chisels and planes. Your saws I advise you to hand over to your nearest 'saw doctor'; most ironmongers are agents for this job. You grind and sharpen your chisels according to the material you are going to cut. For instance, if you were cutting stone or a similar hard material you would use a cold chisel sharpened as in figure 3, with a very short bevel; this is driven into the material with a hammer, and will stand up to a reasonable amount of work before it needs resharpening. If you were cutting the hair on your face, the razor would be ground at a very long angle and no hammer would be required. In other words, less pressure is needed if the angle of your blade is long, giving a fine cutting edge, but of course this fine edge would not stand up to much hammer work before you began to break up the edge of your tool. So we have a choice: using a moderately short bevel and a hammer or mallet, or a longer bevel giving a fine and sharper cut and shearing our material with hand pressure. In most restoration work one needs this moderately long bevel, as shown in figure 4; although in most cases we are cutting fairly hard material, e.g. old mahogany, walnut, etc., we are only shearing off very thin sections as we are cutting very accurately. For instance, cutting a piece of old sawn-cut veneer or a piece of solid wood of the eighteenth century to fit accurately into a damaged part, we have to take off very thin cuts until the piece of wood is exactly the correct size to fit the piece we have cut out from the original damaged part.

This principle applies to both chisels and planes to get the best clean cut on old wood.

I always make a practice of sharpening my tools on the oil-stone at exactly the same angle I have ground at. This may take the beginner some time to get used to, holding the blade of the tool at the same angle all the time, but once you do this you do not have to grind the tool again on the grindstone, but use only your oil-stone. Only if you should damage your edge accidentally need you regrind, and a reground edge never holds up as long as an edge on a tool that has been only oil-stoned for some time. Grinding, I think, opens up the grain of the steel, and the edge of the tool that has not been ground for some time seems to harden with age and become more

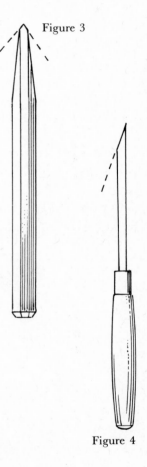

Figure 3

Figure 4

45

durable, and will go on cutting without resharpening for a much longer time. I have discussed this point with engineers many times and they do not agree with me, but this is my experience, and I think most wood-carvers would agree with me. They dislike regrinding their tools, and very seldom do.

To make it quite clear to my reader, I will divide sharpening into three phases: grinding, sharpening, and honing. Grinding is done with an abrasive wheel, usually motor-driven, known as a grind-stone. Sharpening is done on abrasive stone lubricated with oil; these are obtainable in various grades, but usually one has a coarse and a fine oil-stone, the coarse one if your tool is in poor condition (for instance, if you have been cutting some gritty material the edge of your blade will be very rough), a fine oil-stone if your blade is just dull or blunt.

A hone can be a piece of leather rather like the old razor strops, which were used with very fine abrasive paste applied to the leather, or if you want to get mechanised, you can use a motor-driven hard felt wheel treated with a fine abrasive paste. This honing will actually polish the steel, taking off any burr left from the oil-stone and producing a still finer edge, rather like a razor.

Cleaning up applied fretwork *The Antique Collector*

CHAPTER FOUR

Your First Restoration Jobs

A MAHOGANY CHEST OF DRAWERS

I would now like to take you on your first restoration job. You could choose a Victorian tea-caddy or box or perhaps an odd chair, but I suggest starting on a chest of drawers because these are always more in need of maintenance and restoration than most pieces. I imagine most of my readers will have one somewhere, and whether it is a Victorian mahogany chest or an eighteenth-century piece the approach is the same.

First, take out all the drawers and turn the carcase upside down (on a cloth or sheet of course). Now look inside the carcase for any pieces of veneer, beading or inlays etc. that may have fallen from any of the drawers when turned upside by removal men in the past, or pieces put in the drawers by maids or housewives when knocked off by brushes and brooms. Many of these pieces land up behind the bottom drawer and can stay there for a very long time. Do remember how important it is to keep any scraps of original wood, however small. Indeed, it is important in the furniture-restorer's workshop never to throw away any raw materials. Old screws, locks, hinges, nails – in fact almost everything that comes off old furniture – should be saved. New things cannot replace the old for our job. Any metal work is better repaired than replaced, and of course keep every scrap of old wood. There is no waste of wood in restoring; every scrap has a use.

Now get the vacuum cleaner to work inside the carcase and on the bottom of the chest while it is upside down. This will not only remove dust and dirt but will also expose any worm holes that may be there. Now vacuum the back. The chest will be mounted either on bracket feet or a plinth. In either case look for any loose glue blocks; these are the small blocks of soft wood which reinforce the feet or plinth. (If the chest is on turned legs this will not apply.) Having glued any loose parts on the bottom, you can now treat it with wormkiller if this is necessary. I must stress the importance of gluing *before* treating for woodworm because otherwise the chemical in the worm treatment will prevent adhesion of the glue. It is quite safe if the gluing is done first.

A glue block should fit accurately to the corner. Fit each block separately and make sure you have a perfect wood-to-wood contact before applying glue to the block, and then rub the block half an inch or so backwards and forwards until you have squeezed all the glue out from the joint. You will find that after a few rubs the block will put up a resistance. That means your joint is good (see figure 5).

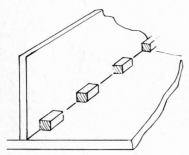

Figure 5

We can now put the chest on its feet again and look for any loose pieces of veneer and moulding that need to be glued. Having satisfied ourselves that everything is firm, we can think about the replacement of those little chips and pieces of veneer that are missing.

The best way to decide on the correct wood for your particular job is by cutting a piece of the original (see illustration) ready for your repair piece to go in, and then from the piece of waste you have of the original you will be able to see the colour of the wood and if it is close-grained or has any other characteristics. In other words, use this piece of original as your pattern and match it as nearly as possible. You will find quite a lot of variation in the colour of old mahogany, and of course a variety of different grains, from open plain grain to figured and close-grained. This can be recognized much more readily in good daylight; artificial light can give quite a different appearance to old wood.

Having found suitable material for your repair, the next thing to watch for is the direction of grain, and to make sure you follow the exact direction of the grain in the original (figure 6).

At this point, I will introduce one golden rule: never cut away more of the original wood than is absolutely necessary to execute the repair. The student will appreciate this point more when he has completed the full restoration of the piece he is working on. When the surface of the piece has been chemically restored to its original colour, he will find that every fraction of the original surface is so valuable in antique furniture that he cannot afford to lose any more than the minimum in the course of repair.

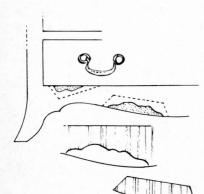

Figure 6

A good restoration job will show little or no sign of restoration when the work is finished, and thus the beauty and value of the piece is enhanced. A good restorer will always be judged by the expert on this basis, so the original should always be preserved as far as possible.

Figure 6 shows the different methods of joinery used to preserve as much of the original as possible, still working on the carcase of our piece of furniture.

48

Now we come to the drawers. Take one and turn it upside down on your bench and you will see the drawer runners are often very thin at the ends through constant use. These runners are usually pieces of oak, about $\frac{3}{4}$ in. wide and $\frac{1}{4}$ in. thick, glued in the recess between the drawer bottom and the drawer side. By prising with a sharp chisel under the joint from both directions you can usually break this joint, or at worst you can gently chisel away all the old runner until the recess is left clean and ready to receive your new runner. To make the new runner, get some old oak that has been used in furniture before. You will find that this oak is a biscuit colour, compared with the white of oak from the timber yard. With the drawer still upside down on the bench, take the width and thickness of the drawer at the nearest point to the front of the drawer. Little or no wear will have taken place at this point. Cut and plane your strips of oak to slightly more than this size, to enable you to take a few shavings off after the runner is glued in and so make the fit to the carcase more exact. In other words, you are replacing exactly what was there before the wear had taken place (figure 7).

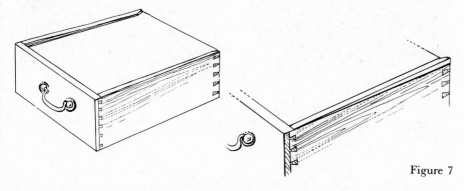

Figure 7

There is an alternative method which can be used if the wear on the runner is not too severe. Plane a straight joint on to the existing runner and apply a piece of oak of suitable thickness, making a good joint surface, to the existing drawer runner and then glue straight on, using G cramps for holding down until the glue is set. This additional piece can then be planed down parallel with the drawer bottom, leaving just a wedge-shaped piece applied to make up for the part worn away, and leaving some of the original runner still on the drawer.

You will find that if the drawers are well worn, a certain amount of wear will have occurred in the carcase itself, and the veneer on the carcase face will also be worn down (figure 8). This means that you will have to replace the piece of veneer that has been worn away, but before doing this you will need to build up the pine or oak where the wear has taken place. To do this, it is necessary to make two thin saw cuts with your dovetail saw just beyond the width of the wear on one side and up to the end of the chest on the other side, taking

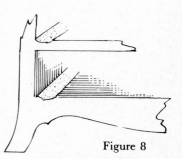

Figure 8

49

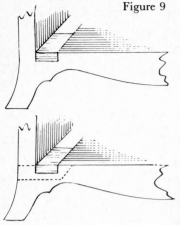

Figure 9

the saw down to the level of the damage in the front, and not less than one inch in towards the back of the carcase. This piece can then be chiselled out to make a flat joint for you to glue your replacement piece onto (figure 9). Then as with the drawer runners, you can level down after the glue is set. This is best done with a chisel or possibly with a bull-nosed plane. The blade of a bull-nosed plane is the full width of the plane, thus allowing you to plane right up close to the inside of the chest end. This means that when levelled down, you have only applied a tapered or wedge-shaped piece, but you have finished up with a level floor for your drawer to run on, and a solid backing for your veneer repair.

The next most serious trouble will find on a chest of drawers is damaged or missing cock beads. These are the beads running round the edge of the drawer face. The short pieces of bead on the ends of the drawers usually suffer most, and it is usually advisable to replace the whole bead. But in the case of longer beads, it is best to cut into the bead and replace only the damaged part.

To make a cock bead, it is simpler in most cases to take a piece of an old dining-table leaf, or any mahogany about $\frac{3}{4}$in. thick, and with your circular saw cut off some strips about $\frac{1}{8}$in. thick. This will give you pieces $\frac{1}{8}$ by $\frac{3}{4}$in., which is usually large enough for beads. Now plane down to size to match the original heads. A sharp scraper can be used to cut the radius on the edge of the bead, which should be a true half circle (figure 10). Finish off with a very fine sandpaper.

There are many fine grades of garnet paper available today, but do not use any coarse-grade abrasive paper. This only scratches the wood, and then you have to take out all the scratches before you can get a good finish.

When cutting in pieces of veneer to restore pieces missing, first match your wood for colour when cut, because when you replace these missing pieces you will have to level flush each piece with a scraper and then fine abrasive paper; so cut your pieces of veneer just slightly thicker than the original to allow for this levelling after the glue is thoroughly hard. If you have to cut these pieces from solid wood, this is a fairly simple job working against the fence of your

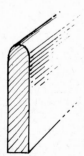

Figure 10

50

circular saw for small pieces at whatever thickness you require, but it is usually possible to find small pieces of veneer of the right thickness off old furniture.

When cutting in a patch the layman may find it easier to cut a piece of veneer to cover the damaged area to a minimum, and then use this piece as a template to mark out what is to be cut away in order to make a tight fit of the replacement; in other words, mark round the edge of your prepared patch of veneer with the corner of a sharp chisel or knife and then cut out the shape of the patch and you should have a good fit, if you cut accurately to the marks. A slight taper can help you to get a perfect joint particularly on end grain as in figure 11.

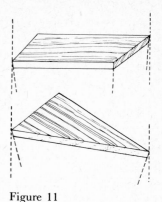

Figure 11

When you have finished all your woodwork repairs you can then go over all the raw wood parts caused by flushing in patches with a piece of solid beeswax rubbed well into the grain; when you are satisfied the grain is filled, take a very fine abrasive paper and gently grind off any surplus wax that remains on the surface of the wood, so that you finish up with a smooth, filled surface ready to receive stain or polish according to the colour of your piece. This base preparation usually applies to all repair work where the polish surface has to be disturbed. If you prepare this surface, flushing and filling properly, it leaves very little to do on the finishing side of the work which I have explained under restoration of colour and surface.

THE TABLE: REPAIRING A RULE JOINT

Repairing a rule joint is quite tricky. This is the moulded joint that appears on most eighteenth-century tables with flaps; the hinges are concealed on the underside of the table and are known as 'back flaps'. These are cut into the table and the leaf in such a manner as to bring the centre of the pin of the hinge exactly in the centre of the radius of the round moulded edge, as shown in figure 12. This means that the knuckle of the hinge has to be cut quite deep into the underside of the moulding, in some cases within $\frac{1}{16}$in. of the outside of the moulded edge, and this is usually where the break occurs, often caused by grit or some small foreign matter getting in the rule joint itself and preventing the leaf from sliding round the moulded edge accurately. Strain is then thrown on to the weakest part where the hinge is cut into the moulding.

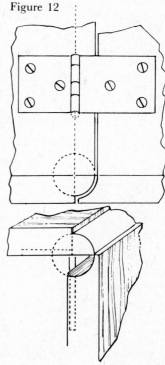

Figure 12

To repair a rule joint you must take the top off the table. This is usually held on by screws on the underside of the frame. Then take the hinges right off to expose the damaged area, which is usually not much more than the width of the hinge; we have to cut back at least $\frac{1}{2}$in. from each side of the damaged part to make a good flat joint to glue the new piece of wood on to, as illustrated. Once the glue is hard we can then carve the new piece to match the curve of the moulded joint from the top, and then turn the top over and recut the recess piece to take the knuckle of the hinge. Go very carefully here and use the hinge cut out next to you as a guide because you

51

will be gouging out a slot for this hinge knuckle from underneath, and coming within a fraction of an inch of the outer shape of the moulding. Once this is done try the position of the hinge and make sure the knuckle of the hinge is just clear of the wood, so that when the hinge is folded there is no friction on the piece of wood left covering the view of the hinge from the table top. This is the piece you have just replaced. Even when you have screwed back your hinge, lift the flap very carefully and slowly and if you feel any resistance it will probably mean you have not cut away quite enough wood to clear your hinge properly. If you force your flap up you will break away the piece you have made good, just as the piece of grit or foreign matter did in the first place.

Finishing off a replacement on a cabriole leg

52

CHAPTER FIVE

Walnut Furniture

Late seventeenth-century and early eighteenth-century furniture I have always treated slightly differently from the later periods simply because of the colour problem. In early walnut veneered furniture there is always a depth of mellow faded colour which is extremely difficult to copy, particularly in the Queen Anne period where most restoration work consists of replacing small pieces of cross banding, feather banding, etc. all over the piece of furniture, thus making bleaching of all these pieces rather impractical, mainly because of the risk of disturbing the original colour next to the repair, and in general spoiling the effect of the whole. This type of walnut furniture has some of the loveliest colours one can find in furniture today. Originally walnut veneered furniture was of a rich brown colour with violent markings in the grain. If we cut the veneer of Queen Anne furniture with a scraper or chisel we would have the richly figured grain almost black in some places, which would be quite the opposite of what we are trying to preserve. This is why I offer you the following technique for walnut.

The basic rule is to work everything backwards: that is, cut the underneath of the veneer when thicknessing ready for your repair, so as to leave the old surface untouched; thus your piece of veneer is fitted quite flush to the old surface and then glued in so that no levelling is done afterwards. If you have matched up your piece of veneer for colour correctly, apart from a final wax polishing no further attention is required. This is also a method that is suitable to early walnut in finish, because there is so much crossgrain work in the bandings, etc., that shows the joints and uneven contours due to shrinkage over the years, that even if your work is not quite accurately flush it can still match the untouched surface of the

53

original. If it were exactly flush and flat in this particular period it would be quite wrong. So this type of repair work gives us quite a bit of licence as far as the replacement of veneer goes.

On the crossgrain mouldings of walnut furniture one can sometimes be lucky and find among the breakers sections of mouldings to match, but most likely it will mean making the moulding in solid walnut. The best approach to this is to examine first the original moulding for thickness and width; examine the crossgrain walnut only, not the pine backing supporting the moulding which is invariably secured to the carcase of the piece, and it is the pieces of cross-grain that get knocked off. Take a board of walnut of the required thickness and cut off from the end grain strips to the width of the moulding to be replaced, usually about $\frac{3}{4}$in. When you have cut a number of pieces (a few more than you need is advisable) glue these to the edge of a softwood board in the same order to match the moulding you are about to make, so that you now have a fair length of crossgrained wood consisting of short pieces jointed together on a softwood backing. Now with the aid of a marking gauge, chisel and gouges you can carve out your moulding to match the original. This piece you have made can now be cleaned up and bleached if necessary and polished to match the original while it is still on the edge of the softwood board, and when you are quite satisfied you have a match to the original it can then be removed from the board, either by cutting it off from the softwood, or removing by heat and melting the glue. When gluing the sections of crossgrain wood on to its backing, have your glue fairly thick and do not make your joint too good; it is then much more easily removable. Once you have taken your moulding off its backing you will have a lot of short pieces of moulding and by mixing these up a little there will be a slight irregularity when glued back on to the pine backing of the original, which in all probability will match the original much nearer than had you worked the moulding on the carcase itself; and of course your moulding is already polished, as in the case of replacement of old surface veneers, so this way you do not disturb any of the original surface and you have little or no polishing to do once your repairs are finished.

Working with old surfaces to match the original can take a little longer the reward is great and I would not dream of treating walnut any other way; this way the repair is seldom seen and the piece never suffers from the 'over-restored' look which can so easily ruin early walnut. If you require replacement feather banding, or herring-bone as it is often called, and you cannot find old replacement material, again you can make up your feather banding in solid wood and then cut into veneers afterwards to the thickness of veneer required. First check the angle of the original feather banding; this is important because they do vary quite a bit from piece to piece in walnut. You can then take a board of walnut (very straight grain) and cut across the board at an angle to suit your next

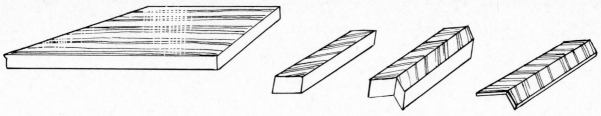

cut, for direction of grain. Once you have established this you can continue to cut off pieces parallel to this in the width you require for the half feather (see figure 13), then by turning over one piece and jointing it to the next with glue you will have pieces of feather banding made to the size you require, up to perhaps $\frac{3}{4}$in. thick, or whatever your board was in thickness. Now if you turn this on to its edge you can cut off the thickness you need and get many pieces of feather banding from each piece you glued up. Once you have checked for correct thickness you can do as before with crossgrain mouldings – clean up and polish ready for your replacements.

Figured walnut is sometimes liable to develop blisters in its veneers, particularly in burr walnut which is of course full of knots and whirling grains which put up quite a resistance the glue, so as the glue perishes a little this lively wood releases itself. To solve this sort of problem is a question of getting more glue under the lifting piece of veneer. If the blister is broken it means dirt has probably got in and will have to be removed before any glue can be introduced. This can usually be done with the aid of a small pencil brush and the thin blade of a knife, but of course if you have an air compressor and a fine jet this can prove very useful to blow out all the dust that may have accumulated under a piece of veneer. Finally, if you can squirt hot water under the veneer, this will soften up the rather stubborn veneer and make it much more pliable to re-lay. The best time to reglue is while the veneer is still damp, the blister can then be put down with very little pressure and held until the new glue is dry. If you have an unbroken blister it will be necessary to make a small cut to enable you to get the glue under, cleaning underneath will not be necessary now, but the hot water treatment will help you to re-lay the blister more easily.

Figure 13

CHAPTER SIX
Oak Furniture

Furniture of the early oak period, that is pre-eighteenth century, is in a class of its own, because of its different construction and the age of its wood. For instance, if you were to compare a sixteenth or seventeenth-century oak stool with turned legs with a late eighteenth century mahogany stool with turned legs, the early oak stool could have odd flats on the turnings and many chips off the feet and legs of the turnings, and still look quite acceptable; a mahogany stool of a later period would look terrible if it had the same amount of damage and would immediately need restoration work. I have to point this out because a slightly different approach is needed in restoration of these earlier periods. If we were to use the same methods on this class of furniture as we do on mahogany, we would finish up with a very new looking piece of furniture.

Because of the great age of some oak furniture, and the everyday use to which it was put, many of the corners and edges are worn away, especially lower rails of chairs, stools and tables as a result of damage from boots and shoes through the ages. The damage has usually been worn smooth by dusting and polishing over a long period, and the colour is also mellowed in these areas. We accept this and even like it because it tells us something of its age, but were it to occur in late mahogany furniture it would simply tell us that the piece had been terribly abused during its comparatively short life and its charm would be lost. I make this point in order to avoid over-restoration, so bear this in mind when working on early oak furniture even more so than the later periods and allow for its age; only repair and replace those parts which may otherwise be an eyesore.

One very distinguishable feature we meet in oak is the dowel pins.

These are the oak pegs that are driven through the tenon joints in order to lock the joint. If you look at an original piece you will find that the pegs or dowels protrude above the surface quite proudly and are never flush to the surface. This is because the wood has shrunk across the width of the grain and hardly at all in the length, and the dowel was made with the grain running in its length: thus we have no shrinkage this way, but the rails or top or whatever board the dowel went through would have shrunk considerably in thickness owing to its age, leaving all dowels standing proud of the surface. So if you do have to replace the dowel, do copy the original and do *not* flush it with the surface or you will spoil a good feature.

For the repair of oak furniture use the same procedure of matching your 'cut wood' colour, and good joinery. The first difficulty you will meet after flushing the surfaces of any replacement pieces will be colour. Most early oak goes in colour from a deep warm brown fading to almost a silvery grey which you will lose as soon as you cut the surface in any way. The bleaching processes mentioned on p. 81 will help to recover the surface colour of the area disturbed, but first I would try using ammonia. This will seem to darken the wood at first, but when dry it will become mellow and grey, and if not quite pale enough in colour can be followed by oxalic acid. When dry apply clear wax polish which will tend to make the wood mellow and faded. If you should finish with too pale a colour the wood will readily absorb coloured wax polish which gives you the chance to tone down to the colour you require.

Another point to remember is that no abrasive papers were used on this furniture when it was made and tool marks can readily be seen on most pieces of this early date. Copy the character next to you on the piece you are working on: it is so simple if you remember this rule and are very observant. Suppose you are replacing a carved panel (perhaps destroyed by worm) in an early oak chest or coffer and its design is of the typical roundel carving. This was originally drawn out with a compass, and therefore geometrically true when made, but with shrinkage over the years it will probably now be a distorted oval in shape. So you would take a rubbing from the neighbouring panel and carve a similar shape for the replacement, and your restoration would be in harmony with the piece. If we were replacing a rail or leg or any other part in an early oak piece we would take note of the warp and distortion that may have taken place and again copy this character of the piece. In other ways we follow the same principle of restoration as described for other periods.

CHAPTER SEVEN
Repairing Chairs

Loose and rickety chairs are a common trouble and the only way to deal with this problem is to take the chair to pieces in order to clean up and refit all the loose mortice and tenon joints. Often you will find that some misguided person has put nails or dowels through the mortice and tenon joint; in this case a wooden dowel can be drilled out but a nail or panel pin can cause a little frustration if the head is driven in flush with the wood. The only way you can cope with this is to lever the rail to one side and insert a small hard wood wedge in the gap you have made on that side of the tenon shoulder; then lever back in the opposite direction pressing against the wedge. This will force the tenon out a little further and allow you to put a wedge in the other end of the shoulder and by repeating this operation the tenon is slowly drawn out from the mortice and will draw the nail or pin out with it. You are using enormous pressure in this lever action, and it must be controlled, so that no sudden breakage can occur.

A good point to remember when reassembling a chair is to assemble the front framework and the back framework separately. After gluing all the tenons, cramp up with iron sash cramps, remembering to put some flat pieces of soft wood between the iron shoe of the cramp and the polished surface of the chair. When the glue is quite dry on these joints you can assemble the side rails to the back and front frames which you have already glued up. This way you will not be confused by having cramps in all directions at the same time.

When you have tightened up a chair frame that has a loose seat you may find that the seat frame will not go in, now that all the joints of the chair are back into their original position. Often one cover after another is put on to a loose chair seat in order to make the seat fit the chair when all the joints have been open; this means you will have to take off any surplus covers under the top cover in order to get the original fit.

I will not go into upholstery in this book because this is a trade of its own and most restorers send their upholstery work to a professional. Changing a seat cover is quite permissible and needs no explanation from me; if you can take a cover off, then I'm sure you can put one on. The changing of seat covers is frequent and one very rarely finds a chair with an original cover.

Re-fitting fretwork panel to a mahogany breakfast table *The Antique Collector*

59

CHAPTER EIGHT

Decorated Furniture

Painted furniture is in a class of its own. In age and design it can compare very favourably with polished furniture, and is in many ways similar in construction and design. But its design is enhanced by cleverly painted lines and motifs, and of course its beauty is heightened by its colouring. The floral decoration in artist's colours, the acanthus leaf and other leaves in shades of green, showing relief similar to carving, and all the other motifs used by the carvers, can all be very attractive; even carved paterae are copied in paint with a delightful effect. Restoration of painted furniture is skilled work as so much of the paint can be flaked off with age. The paint will deteriorate mostly through being in the wrong conditions, too dry or even too damp for a long period, with sudden change causing violent shrinkage or expansion of the wood under the paint, making the paint give way and fall off. When this stage of deterioration is reached, there is often only one solution left and that is to repaint. I have no objection to this, if the piece of furniture is painted in the style and manner of the original, because painted pieces were often repainted several times by experts who invariably kept the style of the original but often changed the layout and design of the decoration. Only on the finer pieces will you find the original decoration as a rule. I do object strongly when I see eighteenth-century decoration on a nineteenth-century piece of furniture. Even late eighteenth-century decoration is so different from the earlier work; the later work is much heavier and much more simple, introducing more gilt work with heavier motifs.

Again we must carry out our restoration principles and copy what we have next to us. In painted furniture it is usually colour and design we are concerned with, but if the base paint of the piece on

60

which the decoration is applied has been chipped or damaged, then we must attend to this first. There may be many layers of paint building up the surface for the decoration to go on to, and if these are chipped they will need filling to bring our final touching-up paint flush with the old surface.

There are many fillers on the market today that might do this job, but I prefer a gesso base. Now for this all you need is whiting mixed with a size or very thin glue. This will make a paste that you can use to fill all the indentations caused by chipping paint. This water solvent type of putty will set reasonably hard and yet can be rubbed down with a very fine abrasive paper or wiped off with a damp cloth should you get any on where it is not wanted. Once you have painted over the filler this tends to reinforce it and there is little chance of it coming out after that. Now you have a level surface where the chipped paintwork had previously caused indentations, and paint work can begin over the white filler.

This is where your eye for colour is important as you have to match up the new paint to the old base colour. This must be done to perfection or else you will have a very spotty complexion on your base colour. If you have matched your colours well you will see little trace of the damage when finished. You can now move on to the decorative features, once your base is dry. The paint on the decoration will be quite thin as this was painted on as an artist would paint a picture, so most of it would be only one brush coat thick. This means you can usually paint in any missing decoration in the normal way without the filling which is needed on the base coat where many coats of paint were used originally to build up a good surface. The paint you use can be artists' oil colours with terebine as a medium; this is a paint-drier used by old-time decorators when they made up their own paints. Terebine will accelerate the drying of your paint and at the same time make the paint very hard and thus a nearer match to the old paint which has hardened with age. The normal bristly brushes used by artists working in oil paints are not suitable; you will need fine camel-hair brushes for this work, as your paint will be much thinner than most artists use because you have added the paint-dryer, which is a very thin medium. I am afraid I cannot tell you how to paint; I can only remind you again to copy the style and colour of what is next to you, providing that you have some of the original to help you. Once all the paintwork is thoroughly dry and hard you will find that the terebine drier has made your new paint rather shiny and it therefore stands out like a sore thumb; the answer to this is to take a fairly soft shoe brush and some fine pumice powder. Brush the pumice powder on all the new paintwork with a fairly light touch and you will produce a completely matt surface. If by chance your old paintwork has a slightly polished appearance you can then by light brisk rubbing with a soft duster usually produce enough polish to match it. If you find that still you need more of the old polished appearance on your new paint, then a light brushing with a shoe brush that has had wax polish on it will usually give the results you need. I say 'has had' because this old wax polish brush will have dry wax-coated bristles and will deposit this wax on your paint and give the extra polish you need. *Do not* apply wax polish direct to your new paint because the solvent used in the wax polish will tend to attack your new paint and as a result you could rub off all your highlights and ruin the appearance of the painting.

Most decorated-furniture artists made very good use of lining – both fine and broad lines in paint or in gold to frame out panels for centre decoration, or to follow along the flowing sweeps of chair legs, rails and backs, or to panel off borders on tables and cabinets for floral decoration etc. If you were redecorating a piece of furniture, you would have to do all your lining first before you moved on to the freehand work. For this you need a steady hand and a keen eye and a lining brush to suit the width of line you are painting. A lining brush has very long hair and is used by filling hairs with just the right amount of paint, not too little and not too much, so that it will not flood your line and make it too wide and will not run out of paint before you reach the end of your line. The brush is used by laying the hair of the brush almost flat against the surface and then pulling it along, leaving a straight line behind it. I am afraid experience is the only teacher for this work. I find I always hold my breath when I am painting a straight line, and the faster you can conveniently move your brush the better the results.

Fitting a new leg to a sofa table *The Antique Collector*

CHAPTER NINE

Damaged Gilt Work

It is not possible here to teach all the various methods of gilding, but the restorer must be able to make good his gilt work on repairs and replacements, so he must understand the principles. He can then adopt his own methods to suit the piece in question and match the condition of the gold on the piece he is restoring. For instance, some of the old gold leaf on furniture has retained its bright metallic finish while on other pieces, perhaps because of the conditions where the piece has been kept, it is of a much more dull appearance; the latter is much more simple to copy, as you will realize once you have tried to produce a bright metallic finish in gold leaf.

First one must prepare a very smooth hard base for the leaf to go on to. This is done by applying a coating of gesso which is a mixture of whiting and size. If you have replaced a piece of carving of a gilt piece of furniture, this raw wood would then need a coat of gesso first in order to build up the hard smooth surface needed, and if copying the original one would have to carve a little deeper to allow for the coating of gesso being applied to the new work. The next step is the base adhesion for the gold leaf. Again check the original but in most cases you will find the base colour is red, which tends to throw up a richer gold. For this use gold size and a little artists' oil-colour paint, to match the original base colour, and apply a thin coat of this over your gesso, remembering that the smoother your base gesso and higher glaze from your gold size the more metallic will be the appearance of your gold. This of course means there must be no dust, as every particle will tend to dull the gold leaf.

To apply gold leaf we have a choice of loose leaf or transfer leaf, the latter being easier to handle. In making good over small areas of gilt work, once the base of the work is ready, the transfer gold leaf can be applied by slight finger pressure over the paper backing causing the leaf to adhere to the work, leaving the paper in your hand.

The gold size base must be thoroughly hard before burnishing can be done. The reason for burnishing is to give a final metallic finish with the appearance of solid gold. This is done with agate, the hard smooth surface of which tends to flatten or stretch the gold leaf to give a bright finish. A piece of perspex or hard plastic with a smooth finish on the working end can also give very good results. To illustrate this, take a piece of metal foil as used in cigarette packets place it on a flat surface and smooth it with your finger, by doing this the metallic brilliance of the foil is restored.

Once this is thoroughly dry and hard the gold can then be burnished; but often in restoration work, with careful application one can match the original without burnishing. The secret is to let your gold size reach a fairly dry state before applying the gold leaf, and if no dust has been allowed to fall on the work before the gold size is dry then this glaze can transfer itself through to the gold leaf and give the results you need. If you look at any gold lettering on glass you will find a brilliant gold because of the hard smooth base of the glass. This example illustrates the principle that the gold leaf has taken up the shape of the surface it is laid on, smooth and polished. If you prepare your base carefully and keep it free of dust you can produce a good gilt finish.

This method will work well on small areas one usually meets in restoration, but in the case of very large areas or complete regilding it is a job for the professional gilder.

Queen Anne walnut bureau on hydraulic jack to facilitate repair to plinth *The Antique Collector*

CHAPTER TEN

Marquetry

I will not attempt to explain how marquetry is done because there are many books on the subject and it is a specialised skill. Our concern is restoration work. For instance, you may have a fine marquetry chest or other piece of furniture with pieces of veneer missing because of damage, or heat and damp. Suppose a leaf or any other part of the marquetry design is missing, the simplest method for replacement is to take a piece of thin white paper and make a rubbing of the space where the veneer is out; this can be done by holding your piece of paper taut over the space and rubbing a piece of heelball, soft pencil or even just a grubby finger over the edges of the damage. You will then have an accurate outline of the piece you have to cut. Now gum or paste this template on to the piece of veneer you have selected for your replacement and when quite dry you can cut out this piece quite accurately with a fine fretsaw, the type used for plywood fret-cutting hobbies. The only point to remember is to select a very fine-toothed saw blade as you are cutting very thin material, and if a coarse saw were used you would not get such an accurate cut and there would be a tendency to break your veneers. Care must be taken not only to match up the correct type of wood with the original, but also to have the grain running in the right direction; this you should be able to determine from looking at the design of the original marquetry work. Having cut your piece, remove the paper and test for fit in the damaged part. If you have cut accurately there should be just a trace of your template or rubbing line left on the paper; this will ensure that your piece will be a tight fit. If you find on testing that it will not go in this is a good fault because you can then take a fine wood file and trim slightly until you get an entry. When filing you can slightly taper the

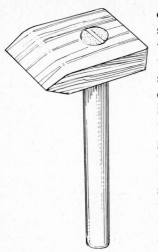

Figure 14

edge of your veneer towards the under surface; this will give you a slight introduction to entry and will tighten up when the piece of veneer is finally pushed home. Do not overdo this slight tapering in the thickness edge of the veneer; it should only be fractionally off square. This is quite possible because of the thickness of the old sawn cut veneers. With fairly thin Scotch glue this piece can now be glued in position. A veneering hammer (see figure 14) can be used to force the new piece down hard on to the base and bring up all the surplus glue, which you can wipe off with a hot damp cloth. If you find that your piece of veneer is slightly thicker and stands proud, you can level this once the glue is thoroughly dry with a cabinet-maker's scraper. These scrapers are flexible enough to bend and thus allow you to level off any proudness of your replacement veneer without touching the original surface, and so finishing quite flush, ready for a very fine abrasive paper and on to finishing.

In marquetry furniture we usually find cross bandings, diagonal banding, etc., and of course box and ebony lines. In the case of bandings, one often finds pieces chipped out, perhaps halfway across the banding or the whole width of the banding; in nearly all cases it is better to cut the piece out, leaving a complete piece the full width of the banding to be replaced. We are then only jointing with the grain and this joint can be invisible if cut in accurately. You should not have much difficulty in cutting in pieces for bandings, but if you are presented with perhaps a curved part or shaped edge you could employ the same principle as with your marquetry patch.

Box or ebony lines are often used to panel off the bandings or to finish the edges of doors, drawers, tops, legs, etc. These are very simple to replace and one occasion when we use new wood. The box and ebony line can be bought in various sizes ready to use straight on to the work. As these lines are usually not more than $\frac{1}{8}$in. square we do not have to worry about their being new wood; when cut as small as this complete drying takes place very quickly and the colour of new box and ebony is very close to old. We can, however, do our final colour balance for box with dyes. When replacing lines on edges make sure that all the old glue has been quite cleared from the tiny recess into which the line sits. When you glue your line in, it will be necessary to hold it there while the glue dries; this can be done simply by using masking tape, and then flushing with a scraper after the glue is set, as we used with the marquetry work. If you find that you cannot match some of the various coloured woods in marquetry work, it is because dyed wood was used quite a lot and in most cases this is sycamore dyed to suit, mostly for the various shades of green, and also other colours where the natural colour of the wood was not suitable.

In restoration work it is usually much simpler to dye your piece of veneer after you have levelled the piece off flush with the original, by applying the dye with a small camel-hair brush carefully over the piece you have just inlaid, and then applying a thin coat of transparent polish in the same way; the colour is then permanently locked in and you have begun to build some surface on the new piece of wood. When the surface of this piece is quite hard, you can rub down carefully with a very fine abrasive paper and apply a second coat; when this is hard a slight rubbing down again and the piece should be ready for building up with a final wax polishing. This would of course depend on what sort of finish is on the original piece; should it be a very high glaze you would have to build up the surface to match, along the same lines I have already mentioned, coating and rubbing down.

Examining repaired splay feet on a bow-front chest of drawers *The Antique Collector*

CHAPTER ELEVEN
Lacquer Furniture

Restoring lacquer furniture is a subject on its own and can be very interesting; yet one does not always need to be an artist, as in the painting of decorated furniture with floral designs. To begin with, most pieces of lacquer furniture that come into the restorer's workshop are dull and dry, usually with coats of perished varnish hiding the gold and coloured decoration below, with chips out of the raised work on the figures, etc. To begin our work we have to make a few tests on an unobtrusive part of the lacquer to find out what solvent we need to remove this perished varnished (see pp. 83-84). In most cases it is usually spirit varnishes that are used on lacquer work, and therefore methylated spirit is the solvent; but great care must be taken because many of the old lacquers are also soluble in spirit and we do not want to disturb the surface below the perished varnish. Do not allow the spirit to remain on the surface of the piece for very long but watch closely as you apply the spirit with a soft cloth, and wipe off immediately the varnish softens. Once you have removed all the old varnish you will be able to see the design of the lacquer work quite clearly and recognize what is missing because of damage. Even if some of the gold work has been rubbed away you will see where the drawing has been so that you can make good when the time comes. It is essential to remember when restoring lacquer, as with most restoration work, that it is far better to leave a little perished surface on the piece than to go too deep when cleaning.

Once you are quite satisfied with the cleaning, the next thing to do is to freshen up the colour so that every detail is visible; this is necessary because in the process of cleaning you will have left a fine deposit of varnish and dirt spread over the surface giving a dull effect. We can overcome this by using a 50-50 mixture of clear

French polish with methylated spirits; this very thin solution is then applied with a camel-hair mop, the type used by French polishers. Brush this solution on as thinly as possible; it will then not leave any heavy deposit over your lacquer, but will simply act as a reviver, leaving the decoration crisp and clear so that you can make good the damage, tracing out any of the original design that is missing.

Once you have a clear picture of the work, the first thing to tackle will probably be the raised work. This often falls away in places because of being kept in wrong conditions such as high-temperature central heating, or dampness followed by heat, or miscellaneous damage. This raised work is done with a raising paste which is a form of gesso. We can make up our own paste with a mixture of whiting and size; whiting is a finely ground chalk compound, and size in this case can be decorator's size or animal glue from the gluepot, diluted with water so that it becomes more of a gum in appearance than glue. This paste can be made up as a thick cream in consistency, or by adding more whiting one can stiffen it into a dough that can be moulded.

For our purpose a thick cream will have a better adhesive quality and can be applied with a small camel-hair brush. Many coats can be applied to build up the thickness required to match the original. In a warm room one coat can follow another as soon as it has stiffened up a bit, which could take anything from fifteen to thirty minutes, depending on room temperature. It is as well to build up the damaged part slightly higher than the original; this will allow for any shrinkage that could take place when hardening, and when hard, say in about eight hours (in a warm room), it is then possible to cut this material with a knife or sharp chisel and also to level down with a very fine abrasive paper, so that it is quite easy to level your new gesso flush to the original. It is important to marry your new material to the old in surface level so that when your paint is applied all trace of the damage will have gone. I use the word paint because this is your next step.

Take a tube of artists' oil colour, 'light red', and use this as your base colour. Mix a little red with gold size, or you could use a coach varnish. In effect you are making a sticky shiny paint, which you will find is very suitable for drawing fine lines and shapes with a small sable-hair brush. With this paint you can paint in all the missing gilt lines, figures, and other decorations. In doing this it is as well to start at the top and work downwards. This is because the gilding will be restored by using bronze powder, and you must keep your fingers away from any of the surfaces of the piece because dry grease from your skin could cause the bronze powder to adhere on these finger marks. The bronze powder is dusted over the red paintwork before the paint is quite dry. The drying again will depend on the room temperature; the paint needs to be caught at the slightly sticky stage because if you allow it to become too dry the bronze powder will not take strongly enough and you will finish up with a rather transparent gold, instead of a heavy full-bodied gold. A piece of soft chamois leather can be used for dusting on the bronze powder, or cotton wool will serve the purpose. The bronze powder is dusted on to the red paint generously and allowed to stand. The next day you can lightly brush off all the surplus bronze powder with a soft brush; a dry two-inch paint brush is ideal for this. Your work should then be allowed to stand for a day or so to allow the paint under the gold to dry out. You can then finally clean off any surplus bronze powder that may have adhered where it is not wanted by a cloth moistened with turpentine, and then wipe off finally with a clean dry cloth to remove all trace of turpentine.

There are many shades of bronze powders, so you must select the powder to match the gold of your original, although the final balance of colour can be done with spirit dyes if necessary. Once your gold work is quite hard, a thin coat of French polish can be brushed over the bronze powder of your gold work. This will insulate the bronze powder and prevent it from tarnishing. A slight colouring can be added to the French polish to tone the gold colour if desired; this can be done by adding a little spirit dye to the French polish, red or perhaps yellow to match the old colour of the original.

There is one point I must mention while we are on gold work. You may find that some lacquer work has been done in gold leaf, in which case to make a good match when restoring you must also use gold leaf. You can use exactly the same procedure as I have stated, but apply gold leaf instead of bronze powder for your gold work.

The next step on gold work will be the black drawing and lining that appears on the figures and leaf work, etc. This can be done again with a fine sable-hair brush, and again use artists' oil colour paint with the addition of terebine. This will give you a very thin paint and thus enable you to draw very fine lines which are called for in lacquer work. If you should find you need a little more body in your paint, the addition of a little coach varnish can be very helpful. This can sometimes help you in drawing a very fine line as the varnish tends to make the sable-hair brush cling to the surface of your work and therefore you can use less pressure on the brush with a resulting finer line. This procedure should be borne in mind when painting on the fine straight lines that are used to panel off the decorative work. For this type of lining, long continuous lines, we need a lining brush, similar to the brushes used by coach-painters and sign-writers. These brushes are made of various hairs and in various sizes for different widths of line. The lining brush is used quite differently from our sable-hair brushes. The lining brush can be anything from an inch and a half to two or three inches in length, but with only a limited number of hairs, giving a long thin brush which is filled with paint and then laid partially flat on the work and pulled along the surface, leaving your line (a narrow strip of paint) behind. This way you can finish up with a nice clean line of even width and with no kinks or bumps.

70

For restoration purposes, all the other colours employed in lacquer furniture can be dealt with by using artists' oil colour and varnish, both on the decorative work and on the ground colour. Artists' oil colours give you every opportunity of matching exactly the old colours of the original and being able to control the thickness of your paint. You will find perhaps that the parts you have done are rather shiny or sticky, but as soon as your work is thoroughly dry and hard you can take off this gloss by lightly brushing pumice powder over the glossy parts with a soft shoe brush. This will dull the new work down to the desired effect and a light friction with a soft duster will bring back the dull gloss which usually appears on old paintwork.

Repairing an 18th Century knife box *The Antique Collector*

71

CHAPTER TWELVE

Inlaid Brasswork and Other Metalwork

Brass inlays which have come adrift in furniture can be a menace in the house: odd pieces of brass sticking out get caught up on the duster and deteriorate each time the piece of furniture is dusted. There are many ways of tackling this problem; if, for instance, the odd piece is sticking out we can clean out the groove or cut out underneath the brass, removing all the dirt, old glue, etc. that has collected there, and then glue the brass in position again, keeping it under pressure with a hand screw and a block of wood until the glue dries. But if the brass inlay has become buckled and damaged through misuse or wrong handling, it will mean taking the piece of brass right out of its housing and then annealing the brass by heating it to a dull red in a flame and then plunging it into cold water. This will make the metal quite soft and pliable. Now we can flatten out any bumps and bends by very lightly hammering them on to a flat metal plate. I must emphasize *light hammering* because if you work this soft brass too much you are liable to spread the metal and make it too large to go back into its housing. It will flatten easily with the minimum amount of effort when it is very soft, and of course will take up its original place in the woodwork of the piece with little difficulty. Scotch (animal glue) is ideal for this purpose and, if need be, one can hold the brass in position with adhesive tape until the glue dries.

If brass work is missing in your piece of furniture, it has perhaps been torn out and lost, in which case we shall need some sheet brass of the same thickness as the original, and again we must anneal this to make it workable. Now we can adopt a similar method to that used in replacing marquetry, by taking a rubbing of the missing part using a piece of thin white paper to make an exact impression. Then paste this to the sheet of brass and cut out with a fret-saw, using the finest blade. If one used a coarse-cut blade the teeth would catch in the thin sheet-brass and chatter badly, whereas a fine-tooth blade will cut smoothly and accurately, leaving very little trimming up with a file to be done to ensure a good fit. Cut very slightly full to the line rather than bare. Only experience can teach you the tolerance you have.

Brass lines on the edges of tables and chairs, etc., are often pulled off and lost. These can usually be bought from reproduction brass-handle merchants in various sizes and it is only a question of cleaning out the old channel where the line is out and cutting the new piece to length; then use the same method of gluing as before. After the glue is dry, final cleaning can be done with a very fine abrasive paper and toned in to match with a little coloured polish. All this brass work was originally cleaned up flush and bright with the woodwork and then polished over the top, and it is this slightly discoloured polish that gives us the old appearance it has today.

Brass mouldings and mounts are usually fixed on with brass pins and very seldom come off, but they do occasionally get loose. A slightly longer pin in the old holes can often overcome this, but if this fails drill a new hole in the moulding and drive in a new brass pin. If the pins are not visible it probably means that the holes have been slightly countersunk and that a countersunk pin has been driven in and filed off flush with the moulding, in which case you can adopt the same procedure. Some of the brass mouldings that occur on furniture are brass-cased and filled with lead from the back, in which case drill right through with a fine drill just giving clearance for your pin. The original pins were usually placed in position in the lead so that no pins were visible, and the moulding itself was hammered to drive the pins into the wood. This type of moulding, usually a half round bead, was used often around the edge of an upholstered seat of a chair, or perhaps on the edge of a table frame on some of the later period furniture.

Boulle furniture, which is inlaid brass and tortoiseshell, can be treated in the same way as described in this chapter, for restoration purposes.

OTHER METAL WORK ON FURNITURE

One needs to understand something about metal because there is quite a lot used in most furniture. All doors have metal hinges of one type or another; many legs have castors; drawers and doors have locks; there are table catches and fasteners, and so on, and most restoration in this field is caused by lack of maintenance. One never thinks of lubricating all these moving metal parts until the bearing of a castor or hinge has dried up and seized solid, so do remember when restoring any piece to lubricate all moving parts that have metal bearings.

If it comes to replacing metal, one usually has to rely on the reproduction-brass merchants and replace with the nearest possible pattern; so whenever possible repair the original. In the case of a seized-up castor, you will usually find a flat spot worn on the wheel caused by the castor being pushed along and not revolving. If the flat spot is not too severe you can take a file and ease off the edges of the flat and marry into the radius of the wheel; then free the bearing of the wheel using a thin oil. The castor wheel will not revolve truly after this but will give a slight bump when revolving.

Many locks often suffer from lack of lubrication and again can be freed by using a thin lubricating oil which will creep in and free the offending part. Door bolts that are hard to operate can usually be freed with a little oil. The other trouble that can happen with bolts is that the hole the bolt shoot goes into becomes filled with dirt or rubbish and prevents complete movement of the bolt. This can happen with door locks as well; in this case it is usually the slot (cut out in the style, or rail, of the piece of furniture) that gets filled up or damaged in such a way as to prevent the shoot of the lock from entering fully into the slot and thus jamming the lock itself by the action of the key. Most drawer and door locks are fairly simple in construction, at least on average pieces of antique furniture. There are of course always exceptions, but in most cases locks are held on by four wood screws and are easily removed. Once off the piece of furniture we turn to the inner face of the lock and usually find two small metal thread screws holding the core plate, sometimes also supported by two small tongues protruding from the case. These can easily be prised up, and so expose the working interior of the lock. All the earlier types of lock found on antique furniture are worked on the ward principle: that is, small pieces of metal protrude from the base of the lock interior and the keys for such locks have slots cut in to correspond to wards in the lock, thus allowing the key to be turned if the key is correctly cut. The key then having passed these wards in its turning is now able to engage the lock bolt, or shoot, and push it forward to lock (figure 15).

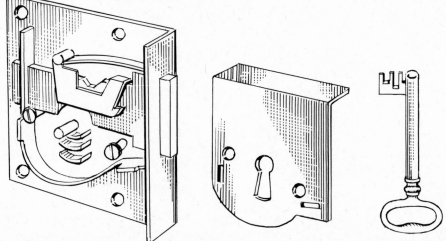

Figure 15

74

The lever lock principle was used at a later date in furniture becoming general in the 1820s and 1830s. The key and bolt principle is still here but instead of the key passing over wards, the end of the key is cut in various shapes (see figure 16) to engage small levers and lift them to a certain level to allow the lock shoot to be thrown forward and backward. These small levers are spring-loaded so as to keep the lock shoot in position until these levers are lifted by the key.

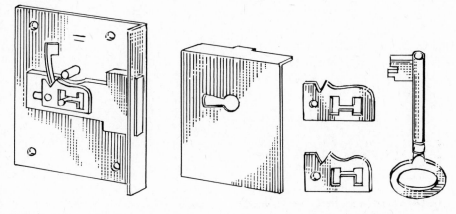

Figure 16

Cutting a key for a ward lock is not too difficult once your lock is dismantled. A key blank of the correct size for the lock can be obtained from most ironmongers; it is then only a case of cutting with a thin ward file the corresponding slots to clear the pieces of metal obstructing the key from entering the lock. This can be accurately cut by smearing a little black lead or graphite on the end of the key so that when you insert the key and move it a little you will produce a polished mark just where the wards are to be cut.

A lever lock is a little more complicated; in this case the control takes place at the end of the key and not at the base, as in the case of a ward lock. The same type of key can be obtained in blank form but we have to file the end of the key in a manner so as to leave a series of small prongs of different lengths corresponding to the amount of lift each lever requires in order to free the shoot of the lock so that it can be pushed forward by the action of the key. The number of prongs required will depend on the amount of levers in the lock. Whether it is a 2, 4 or 5 lever lock, the corresponding prongs will need to be on the key, and of varying lengths so as to give each lever the correct lift, as shown in figure 16.

CHAPTER THIRTEEN

Fretwork

Fretwork galleries and brackets were often made of three-ply woods, the centre section usually vertical grain leaving the two outside veneers long grain. By this lamination very fine decorative pierced work was possible. These galleries were seldom more than $\frac{1}{4}$in. thick, and although quite strong they do come in for considerable damage. When repairing a section of this type of fretwork, it is well to stagger your joints on the three laminations, thus reinforcing each joint you have made by covering with the next veneer.

In the case of a replacement section of gallery, I find it best to cut off with the circular saw from a piece of solid wood of the right type to make veneers to the correct thickness of the original. Thus you get the exact thickness for the gallery when completed, because usually this has to fit into a groove on the table top.

CHAPTER FOURTEEN
Table Lining and Embossing

Table lining in leather can be quite a specialist job, but the restorer must have some knowledge of the subject. The most frequent job that one runs into is the replacement of baize linings of card tables. I have found that every card table that comes in for restoration work needs the baize renewing. The best material for this is billiard cloth, although many of the better quality baizes are quite permissible. One can usually pull off the old cloth without much difficulty; the cloth left on can be washed off with warm water, and at the same time this will dissolve the old paste left on the table under the old cloth. A little scraping may be necessary to get the surface quite clean, ready for relining.

Paperhanger's paste is the best adhesive for re-laying your new cloth. This should be applied generously and brushed in well with an ordinary paint brush and continually brushed until the paste builds up to almost a gum consistency; when it becomes very sticky and not too wet, this is the time to put on your cloth. Cover the whole of the table and let the surplus cloth overhang. Then take a piece of softwood about 2 inches long and slightly round one edge; this is used as a sort of veneering hammer which can be dragged across the cloth to squeeze the paste into the underside of the cloth, so making a perfect seal, rather like laying a piece of veneer. Then take your wooden block round the edge of the table and with a corner you can press the cloth down tight into the recess; finally, by running your thumb nail into this recess you will produce quite a sharp line where your cloth has to be cut. Now, before the paste is quite dry, but held fairly firm, you can run the corner of a sharp chisel, or the point of a knife if you prefer, along this recess and cut off the surplus cloth accurately to the shape of the table.

Lining in leather is done in exactly the same way, with paperhanger's paste and the same method right through, except for one thing which you must watch for: leather will stretch quite a bit when it is dampened by the paste. This can be to our advantage because if your cutting in the edge of the table recess has not been too accurate, by using the softwood block you can work the leather from the middle towards the edge and close up any gap you may have. Both cloth and leather lining should be sealed on the edge by an embossing wheel; this makes a nice finish to the edge and a better seal to prevent any shrinkage of the material from the edge.

The embossing wheel is heated to about the same temperature as the domestic clothes iron; this can vary with experience of handling. This hot embossing wheel must never be applied while the leather is still damp. If you take a small piece of leather and dip it in water and then apply sudden heat to it, you will find it will shrivel up and shrink to almost nothing; so you can imagine what would happen to the edge of your leather top if your wheel was too hot and the leather damp. Only experience can teach you just how much licence one has with leather.

The gilt embossing you find on leather-topped desks and tables is done with a brass embossing wheel, the same as the edging tool, but of course more decorative, and wider designs are used for this purpose. Loose gold leaf used to be cut into strips and laid along the line where the embossing wheel was to travel, with a thin fixing solution that caused the gold leaf to adhere to the leather under the pressure and heat of the wheel. Today this method has been supplanted, as the manufacturers of gold leaf now produce a roll of gold on film that can be fed out by the left hand while the right hand follows behind with the wheel. It is much faster and the result is equally as good as the old method. To use an embossing wheel is a very skilled job. To get a true register of the pattern in your leather you have to rock the wheel from side to side to get the edges in and backwards and forwards to complete the register, while at the same time travelling in a line parallel to the edge of the table, watching all the time that the temperature is correct on the wheel, not too hot or it can burn the gold, and not too cool or the gold will not take. From this complex description you will see that it is really a job for the specialist.

CHAPTER FIFTEEN

Finishing

PREPARATION

I will now assume that you have completed the gluing side of restoration, so we can move on to the finishing. I use the word finishing which is the final process after preparation, or cleaning up, as it is known in the trade; that is, flushing your new piece with the original without removing too much of the original surface. This is done with a smooth plane in the case of a piece of solid wood, followed by the scraper; use only the scraper in the case of flushing veneer. Then, as a final finish, use a very fine abrasive paper. If you run your fingers across the joint while looking away from the piece, you should not be able to detect the joint. Visually the joint may be detected by slight variations in the grain or colour of the wood. It is very important that the join be perfectly flush, because if it is not, no matter how well the colouring or finishing were done, the new piece would still show. This is one of the important principles: perfect surface and contour, as in the original. Then, and only then, can you move on to the finishing stage which includes colouring and polishing.

The first step is to get the colour of your new pieces to match the original, and you may have done this by correct selection of wood in the first place. I give in subsequent sections more detailed instruction on colour, stains and dyes but here follow through the sequence of a typical job.

There is every likelihood that the match will not be exact, and often your new replacement will show up lighter in colour than the original. This means staining or dyeing the piece to match. There are numerous stains and dyes available today, but often the simplest is the best. One stain that has many uses is vandyke crystals, obtainable at all the polish-suppliers, which is a water stain. The crystals are dissolved in warm water, making a solution of a warm brown colour, ranging from honey to dark oak according to how much water is added. This stain is absorbed into the wood, and is quite permanent.

POLISHING

A thin coating of French polish is then applied, either with brush or 'rubber', which is a pad of cotton wool covered with soft white rag and used by French polishers.

To make a polisher's rubber a little care is necessary. The ideal material for this is an old well-washed pocket handkerchief. It is soft, pliable and absorbent and closely woven to give us the smooth surface. Next we need a small wad of cotton wool. Mould this cotton wool into a pear shape, and place in the rag; now fold the cloth from the front end of the rubber so as to tighten it almost to a point, leaving the back end, that is the end towards your wrist, quite loose and free; twist the remainder of the rag round into the palm of your hand, and you should now have a heel and toe to your rubber. If held with your forefinger on the pointed end of the pear shape and the heel of the rubber almost in the palm of your hand, you should have a controllable pad with which to apply your polish.

Now take off the rag to expose the wadding and then pour polish on to the wadding, almost to saturation point; replace the rag with heel and toe shape and twist the surplus rag again into the palm of your hand. This will squeeze out any surplus polish and leave you with a nicely moistened pad with a pointed end to reach into corners, guided by your forefinger, and a soft pad at the bottom which can be pulled lightly over the work you are on. Do not make your rubber too wet or you may cause tears on your work, and do not be too mean with your polish or it will tend to drag. A little practice and you will get the feel of it. Do allow a few minutes between each coat before going over the same ground, in order for the polish to dry enough to prevent being pulled off by the next application. Should you get any streaks in your work, or rubber lines as they are called, a light rub down with very fine wire wool between the coats can often eliminate this.

The French polish acts as a sealing medium, being absorbed into the wood and setting hard, rather in the same way as size is used by decorators for sealing a plaster wall before papering or painting. This polish, which is basically dissolved shellac, will help to fill the pores of the grain and harden the surface of the wood. The surface when hard can be rubbed down with a very fine abrasive paper, and then another coat added. The operation can be repeated several times until the grain appears to be reasonably full. Remember that each time you rub the surface down you are taking the polish off the surface of the wood and leaving a deposit in the grain, so you finish up with a very thin coat on your wood surface, but the grain has now become quite full.

The next phase is wax polishing. There are many wax polishes on the market, but I find that shoe polishes are much better quality than most other types. For anyone who is restoring professionally, here is a good formula for a wax polish which can be used in a more concentrated form.

FORMULA FOR WAX POLISH
Carnauba wax 40%
Paraffin wax 40%
Beeswax 20%

Dissolve on a hot plate and add twice the amount by volume of pure turpentine to the molten wax. Stir while cooling and add more turpentine if desired to thin down. Be careful when heating the waxes as they are highly inflammable.

FADED COLOUR OF FURNITURE
The colour of old furniture is very important. The design is enhanced by the harmony and beauty of its colour.

If a piece of furniture is in untouched condition, or has been restored expertly to look thus, you will find that most of the colour is in the wood itself, particularly if the colour is faded and mellow. That is why with care all the polished surfaces can be removed from a piece of furniture without losing the faded colour of the wood, and then by repolishing correctly we can restore the patina-like finish we desire. The depth of fading in furniture can hardly be measured; it is so thin that any abrasive action, such as that produced by even very fine glass paper or other abrasive paper, would destroy the surface colour immediately. This faded wood effect can be reproduced by chemical means, such as the use of bleaches and acids.

There are many bleaches on the market today, sold mainly by polish-manufacturers using their own formulae, usually offered in two solution packs. Most of these are basically a strong alkali such as ammonia or soda solution or waterglass, which penetrates the wood and releases the dye; this is then followed by the number 2 solution, which is usually 100 vol. peroxide applied just before the first solution is quite dry. This sets up a chemical action and causes the wood to dry out to a pale bleached biscuit colour. Thus we can have a piece of furniture looking like a scrubbed kitchen-table top, but even with all the staining and dyeing available it is extremely difficult to make it look anything like the original, because the drastic bleaching has dulled the beauty of the wood grain and left a cold uniform effect completely different from that of the original colour of an untouched piece. The variety of pastel shades ranges from the palest honey colour through to warmer shades of red and

81

brown and down to vandyke brown and plum in the more shadowed parts of the piece. This beauty cannot be artificially made, any more than you could paint a rainbow once you have seen the original; the beauty of nature is quite a challenge.

However, there are occasions where these strong bleaches can serve a purpose; for instance, if the restorer has replaced a fair sized piece of wood in a faded piece of furniture and is left with a dark patch as a result, then this type of bleach can be useful if handled skilfully, to lighten a small area in colour where the repair has been made, and then with the use of dyes and stains on the bleached area a reasonably good marriage can be effected.

Do not let fine wire wool come in contact with any kind of bleach, particularly oxalic acid. This can give off dangerous fumes and could possibly cause fire. It is quite safe to use wire wool after you have washed off the surface; even on the wet surface there is no danger from the little bleach that may remain.

STAINS, DYES AND PIGMENTS

I have already mentioned the value of vandyke crystals, and how they can be applied to raw wood, but it is also possible to use them on a polished surface, providing you matt the shiny surface first. This can be done with any light abrasive such as pumice powder, fine abrasive papers or the finest grade of wire wool. It is then possible to stain on to a finished surface, with the advantage of being able to remove the stain with a damp cloth to produce highlights on carvings or other prominent parts, and shadowing, etc., thus attaining complete satisfaction with your work before finally fixing with clear polish. A thin coat of polish will penetrate the water stain and adhere to the polished surface below.

There are many other types of stains, such as naphtha, spirit and oil stains, but I find very little use for most of these, except for naphtha, which is soluble in turpentine and therefore useful for the colouring of wax polishes. One can also use turpentine dyes for this purpose. Naphtha stain offers a much more permanent red than other red dyes and stains. I particularly mention this because one often needs a hint of red on parts of furniture, or in touching up, in order to slightly warm up a very cold colour, and if this red were to fade, as some reds are liable to do, we are usually left with rather greenish yellow as a result. I have seen this so often where repairs have been matched in with spirit colours particularly, and these ghastly cold yellow patches develop within six months of being done. Spirit dyes have the advantage of being very powerful and yet transparent, and so can change the colour of a piece of wood without covering up the beauty of the grain, whereas pigments are the reverse in as much as when dissolved in any medium they can obliterate all below, like decorators' paint. Paint is simply pigments dissolved in oil and varnishes and other synthetic media, just as pigments dissolved in water with the addition of size or other fixatives would become suitable for painting the wall of your house as distemper. We use our pigments dissolved in clear French polish to make a paint suitable to use on furniture where we need to obliterate something – perhaps a burn or scar.

It is important for the student to know his colours, and I would strongly advise anyone who is not too sure to take a short course at an art school. By using artists' colours, one can quickly learn how to achieve varying effects by mixing one colour with another. Although the matching of colours on old and faded furniture is much more of a challenge, the colours are very subtle and can be much more exciting. In matching any colour on old furniture, particularly faded colour, one must develop an analytical eye to recognize just what the old colour is composed of. For instance, if you analyse the pale colour of a piece of Queen Anne walnut furniture, at first appearance it is perhaps a golden honey colour, but on closer examination you will find it starts with a base colour of a warm off-white, with pale shades of brown, red and yellow, giving a tortoise-shell effect with the pale base colours breaking through the topmost colours. This means that if you were trying to touch in a serious bad spot on a piece of furniture of this nature you would first have to match your palest colour in the base and then apply the other colours over this base in order to get the same effect. In short, you are copying what is next to you.

RESTORING COLOUR AND SURFACE

First we have to determine what is on the existing surface, and to do this we start off with the mildest solvents, such as warm water and soap or a weak solution of detergent. This will remove all dirt and grease from the surface, but if any parts are a little stubborn you can carefully use one of the domestic abrasive cleaners, or a little fine pumice powder with a wet cloth, when you are washing the piece.

If this first approach does not give what you are looking for, it means that the surface now has old French polish or perished varnish to be removed. For this I suggest that you try methylated spirit. Use it sparingly on a cloth and watch closely to see what reaction you get. Probably it will dissolve the top surface, as you will see by the colour on your cloth, and the difference on the surface if you are going deep enough to expose the beauty of the wood. The important thing is *not* to go too deep, because if you do you will soon see that you are taking the old filling out of the grain and thus on to raw wood, thereby destroying any of the original surface that may have been there.

With all surfacing work, it is essential to let your eye follow your hand so that you observe everything that is happening where you are disturbing the surface, and you are thus able to ease off immediately you have reached the point where the unwanted polish or varnish is removed and yet a thin surface is left on the wood. This is as near as you can get to the original patina, and once the surface is polished you will find that the colour and beauty of the wood will speak for itself.

If, however, this second approach should not be effective, then further tests must be made to find the correct solvent for the unwanted layer we are trying to move. Having tried detergents and methylated spirit with no success, then amyl acetate or cellulose thinners are another possible solvent if any previous coating of cellulose or other synthetic polish has been used. Again, treat the surface cautiously with the solvent on a cloth, as we are still looking for a solvent that will remove only the unwanted surface and not penetrate too deep.

Should none of these solvents attack the old perished surface, then we can be a little more drastic by using one of the well known strippers, and here I suggest a petroleum-based stripper which is very thin and more easily controlled. This very thin petroleum wash can be applied with a paint brush and the reaction can be seen almost immediately. Watching the surface, you will see the old varnish lifting by chemical action, and as soon as you see this old surface erupting evenly all over, then wipe it off immediately with plenty of rags, avoiding rubbing as far as possible as this has a tendency towards an abrasive effect and may take you deeper into the surface than is desirable. If you find some of the old perished surface still left on after your first application, then apply another coat of stripper at once to the area, and again watch for the chemical action: wipe off at once, using one or two clean wipes so as to avoid rubbing. By experience, you will discover just the right moment to remove the stripper, and once you have mastered this you will find how much the finished colour and patina improve on the finished piece.

I must warn you against using any of the more powerful paint-strippers if you intend to recover any of the original colour, as most of these paint-strippers go right through everything and leave you with raw wood with all the grain opened up. I regret to say that this sort of thing does happen, and the French polisher moves in and fills the grain with synthetic wood-filler and then repolishes. The result is a new piece of furniture in appearance, with all trace of the beauty of age gone.

The next stage of surfacing is polishing. This again will need slightly different application according to the piece, but basically the principle is to smooth the surface that we have disturbed. This is done first by a very light rub down with the finest grade of wire wool, usually 0000 grade. Use very little pressure on the surface because all you need to do is to rub off any slight roughness left behind after the stripper has dried out, and as the surface has now hardened again this slight abrasive action will not harm the surface colour. If you have had to use petroleum-based stripper on the piece, a deposit of wax will be left on the surface. This does no harm but in fact it tends to keep the colour of the wood pale, which is to its advantage. The next step is to give the whole surface a thin coat of

84

clear French polish. We are not attempting to French polish this piece, but we are using this clear polish as a sealing or fixing medium (a second coat may be applied if necessary). The polish is basically shellac dissolved in methylated spirit, although all manufacturers have their own formulae with probably various additives. Any good quality clear polish will serve our purpose. Most of this first coat will be absorbed into the grain, and if our cleaning down or stripping has been done well, all we need after this is another slight rub down again with fine wire wool. Use nothing of a coarse nature as this would damage the surface. The fine grade will grind the surface without scratching. After this, the surface is ready for waxing.

Wax polishing is in itself quite a skilled job if done properly. Just applying the wax polish to the surface and rubbing it off again is not the way. The wax needs to be applied very generously and rubbed into the surface and continuously rubbed with the same wax-soaked cloth in a circular motion, rather like a French polisher does when he is 'bodying up' (a term used when building up a surface). We are doing almost the same thing, but with wax. While we are rubbing away with plenty of pressure on the cloth, the solvent in the wax polish is evaporating, and the wax is being deposited on the surface, building up to a hard and durable surface. Keep your wax pad moving while the solvent of the wax is evaporating, as it is this that leaves the hard wax deposit behind. Do not change the cloth with which you are applying the wax, and you will find that it also has a hard deposit of shiny wax, which means that all the solvent has evaporated and the maximum amount of polish has built up. If you applied a second coat immediately, the solvent in the wax polish of your new application would tend to dissolve the wax already built up, and you would not gain much from the second application, so allow a long enough period between the waxings that your first coating of wax will become so hard that it will not readily dissolve again. You will see examples of this in the home of anyone who cares for old furniture and where the furniture is wax polished regularly. The surface becomes quite brilliant with a hard durable shine which has built up over a considerable period of time.

CHAPTER SIXTEEN

Wood-Carving

Wood-carving in restoration work requires quite a different technique from that used by the skilled wood-carver. I have known very skilled carvers do work on a piece of antique furniture that has afterwards been condemned. The reason for this is that each carver develops his own style and is very familiar with all the known motifs – e.g. the acanthus leaf, the shells and scrolls, etc. – which appear in carvings. This is his downfall as a furniture-restorer. Now the furniture-restorer who is basically a cabinet-maker, and so can handle sharp tools of all kinds, will copy exactly what he can see, cut for cut, imitating every motif precisely and matching his carver's tools to the curves and angles of the original carving. In his finished work there will be nothing of his own style. Thus his replacement pieces are much more in harmony with the original, and much less offensive to the eye, than the professional wood-carver's.

Most of the carving which needs restoration is the result of damage, as when pieces are broken off in transit (e.g. leaves, flower petals and other prominent parts of carved motifs) or storage, or perhaps in the home itself; while waiting for restoration, these pieces get lost, and so the restorer one day has to replace them. Another common casualty which entails carving is the edge of a pie-crust table top, as shown in figure 17. In this case you will have to take note of the general design of the pie-crust edge if there is a large piece missing, because you will find that the pattern repeats itself around the edge of the table top, and so once again you can copy what is next to you while following out the correct design of the repeat pattern. These pie-crust tops were always cut from solid wood. The centre part of the top was usually turned out on a lathe, leaving a narrow band of wood standing proud from the top for the

Figure 17

86

carver to cut and shape, as shown in figure 18. This means that approximately fifty per cent of the edge is left of a short crossgrain nature, as the illustration shows. When the carver has done his work we have a delicately carved moulding on the edge of a small round table; should this table get knocked over and fall with the short grain section to the floor this moulding is bound to break off at the point of impact, and of course many of these pieces get lost before someone is able to glue them back in place.

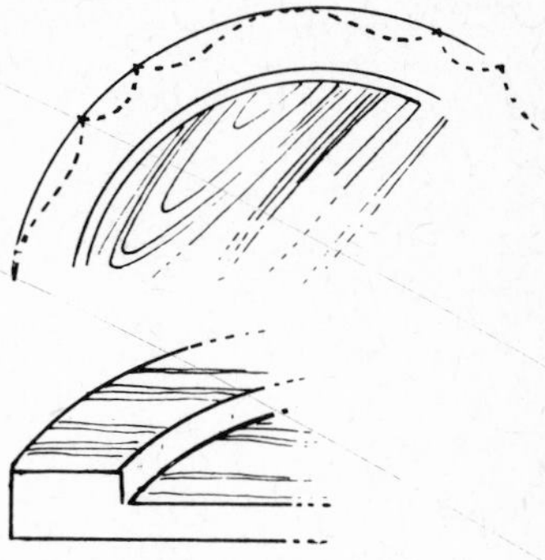

There are many other forms of carving that appear on furniture, such as moulded legs and arms on chairs and moulded chair backs. All these are free hand carvings and suffer damage in many ways, so that pieces have to be let in and carved back to the original moulded shape. There are of course applied carvings such as paterae, which are carved ornaments applied to the face of furniture, which fall off when central heating perishes the old glue. The round patera was usually turned on a lathe and then carved with leaf motifs, but oval and other shapes of patera were entirely free hand. Carved feet and legs often come in for quite a bit of damage. Here we carry out the same procedure, cutting in a piece of wood of the same kind and age and carving to copy the original.

To mention yet another type of carving, there is fluting and reeding which occur on many pieces of furniture and also entail the use of carving tools. Once you are able to use your carving tools you can become a good copyist and a good restorer with very little knowledge of carving. I consider it much more important to understand the age and quality of the piece of furniture you are working on.

Figure 18

CHAPTER SEVENTEEN

Glass

Replacement of glass in decorative glazed doors needs to be handled very carefully because the putty used for the original doors has become rock hard with age and the risk of breaking another pane of glass next to the one you are replacing is very great while you are removing the old putty. The safest way to work is first to take the door off its hinges from the edge of, say, the bookcase, leaving the hinges on the door; this way you will find it much easier to re-hang the door after you have finished the repair. Now lay your door face down on a cloth-covered bench or table so that the putty side of the glass is accessible, and try cutting behind the old putty with an old chisel, tapping the end of the chisel with a light hammer (a light hammer because we cannot afford too much vibration for fear of breaking a neighbouring pane of glass in the case of a multi-pane door). Sometimes the old putty will split away from the frame in hard lumps, but if this method fails the next step is to soften up the old putty with heat. This can be done by using an electric soldering iron and running it along the putty to soften, following with your chisel while the putty is soft. Cleaning out the old putty from the small rebate is the worst part of the job, but once this is done you can cut a new glass to fit the shape of the original pane.

Glass-cutting is not a very difficult job if you start off with a new glass cutter; the ordinary wheel type is quite suitable. In the case of a shaped pane of glass, the professional will lay a piece of glass large enough to cover the area to be replaced and simply cut freehand, following the shape of the frame below. I would not advise this for the beginner but suggest that he makes a paper or thin card template of the shape and lays his glass over this template on a flat bed; then cut with the aid of a straight edge for the straight cuts, and perhaps freehand on the curved lines. This can be done much more easily when working down on a flat bed and not on the door as the professional would.

The only tips I can offer you in using a glass-cutter are first, to make sure you have a flat bed, for instance a piece of thick ply-wood covered with a piece of baize; second, do not press too hard on your cutter, and make a positive stroke; do *not* go back on a cut once you have made it, this can damage the wheel of your cutter and possibly break your glass. If you are cutting a freehand shape you can go quite slowly but positively. If the shape is very intricate you can make cut lines running away on the waste side of your glass in order to remove the waste glass to take the strain off the piece you need. When you have made the cut a gentle tapping on the underside of this thin glass will cause it to run along the lines of your cut and release the piece you require.

In a 13 pane door, or any other 'broken up door' as they are called, the panes are only divided by a thin slip of wood no more than $\frac{1}{8}$in. thick usually, so remember when cutting your glass or template for the glass to allow a little freedom on the size of your glass so that it can drop into the frame without force. You cannot cut away any of the frame if your glass is too light. With an old bookcase door I do not use ordinary putty as used by glaziers, but prefer to use a gesso compound that will set almost as hard as the original, overnight. Mix up whiting with a little size or very thin glue from your pot until you reach a putty-like substance, and while mixing include enough pigment powder colours to match the original colour as nearly as possible (usually brown umber and a little red ochre will match the mahogany colour found in these bookcases). When you have a workable putty put a very thin layer in the bottom of the rebate for the glass and then press your glass down gently but firmly so as to squeeze out any surplus putty and leave just a thin bed for the glass to rest on, after which you can fill in the bevel of putty to match the other panes of glass. When your putty compound is dry you can wipe off any surplus with a damp cloth. You will find that when your putty is quite dry it will look a paler colour; if you take a little transparent polish and apply a thin coat with a small camel-hair brush, this will serve as a sealer for the surface of your putty and will restore the colour to the one you mixed when wet. In working on decorative glazed doors it is well to remember that before the glass was put into these doors they were extremely fragile, and they do rely on the glazing to give them strength; so if you have several panes out at once you will have a very delicate structure to deal with.

CHAPTER EIGHTEEN

Removal of Stains and Bruises

Ink is one of the commonest stains found on old furniture. Fortunately, this does not present much of a problem. Oxalic acid crystals dissolved in warm water and applied to the affected area with a paint brush and allowed to stand will bleach out the ink without doing any harm to the surface of the wood. Once again, very little rubbing is needed – chemical action will do the job for you if you allow enough time.

If, however, someone in the past has put any kind of French polish or varnish over the ink, then the action of oxalic acid is arrested by this insulation. Then it is necessary to remove this coating, and the simplest way to do this is to rub the ink over with a very fine waterproof abrasive paper, while the acid is on the stain. This will allow the acid to seep through and reach the ink.

If these ink stains are on a pale-coloured piece of furniture, after the ink is removed we are left with darker patches of wood where the ink has been. These are caused by the ink protecting the wood from the light and preventing fading. There is no easy answer to this, but one suggestion may help: put a coat of clear wax polish over the area. This will build up the surface you have disturbed, the fading being accelerated by the wax, and in the course of time the dark mark will gradually disappear. It is possible to bleach the darkened area and tone with aniline dyes to match the original, but this is a difficult operation and calls for the touch of an expert.

Other common blemishes to be found on furniture are wine stains and water marks. These are usually the result of spilt water or wine being allowed to dry on the surface, causing the white marks that every housewife grumbles about. The answer to this is to revive the colour which has been hidden by the surface marks, and for this

90

linseed oil is the best medium. Apply it with the tip of your finger and rub over the white mark, using pressure and friction. This action will cause heat and the heat caused by the friction and pressure of your finger tends to soften the polished surface slightly, thus allowing the oil to penetrate and revive the colour. In short, heat and oil are the best agents for reviving colour, no matter how you may apply them.

The method I have given you for white marks on polished surfaces is a simple one and will usually work, but in obstinate cases a more scientific approach may be necessary. For instance, a little methylated spirit with the linseed oil may be used, although with great care as the methylated spirit will tend to soften the polish and allow the oil to penetrate more easily. You must remember that methylated spirit is a solvent and could remove your surface altogether if you are too generous with it. So be generous with your oil, as this can all be wiped off with a cloth as soon as the mark has gone, but be very sparing with the methylated spirit, and allow the surface to harden again as soon as the mark has gone. The surface can be wax polished after forty-eight hours.

While we are willing to accept a certain amount of bruising on old furniture as fair wear and tear, there is sometimes an objectionable bruise showing strongly enough to deface the piece. We can overcome this well enough to be acceptable, although the bruise may not disappear completely but leave a very slight scar. There are various techniques for this. If you wet any wood, it will swell in size, and if the water is warm or hot it will accelerate the action. So a simple method of dealing with most bruises is to apply a wet cloth to the bruise and then with a hot soldering iron push the wet cloth right into the bruise. This will force the steam from the wet cloth into the affected part and cause the wood to swell and lift the bruise up to its normal level. One point to remember is to keep your soldering iron on the move all the time so as not to burn the cloth or the wood. You may need to wet the cloth again several times before the bruise is completely out, and watch carefully to make sure you are putting the steam just where it is required in the bottom of the bruise. When the wood is thoroughly dry, wax polish applied with a shoe brush and brushed briskly across the damaged part will usually build up the surface and marry the affected area into the original enough to satisfy the eye.

CHAPTER NINETEEN
Some Final Thoughts

I have tried to cover as thoroughly yet as simply as possible the whole field of restoration of antique furniture, on the assumption that my reader is a person of good common sense; and if I have shown the basic principles of this work, it is only common sense and initiative, plus some experience, that can put him on the right path.

There is one question that you may be faced with when you do acquire this expertise: where does restoration end and faking begin? This is a difficult one to answer, because you have to become a first-class copier in restoration work, so that your work blends in and harmonizes with the original, and becomes indistinguishable from the original; this I believe is good restoration. And yet, on the other hand, one must limit somehow the amount of restoration permissible before the piece of furniture becomes a fake. For instance, if one were to restore extremely rare piece of furniture, a museum treasure, then one would be justified in going to great lengths in order to recapture this piece for all to see; but if a common piece of furniture were snatched from the scrap heap and nearly remade, then the person buying this piece would be in danger of being deceived if the dealer did not point out its recent history: in my opinion, he would be selling a fake. Apart from this sort of faking, there are of course deliberate fakes made and put on the market; but the good restorer can recognize these pieces every time because he has had experience in copying originals during his restoration work, and if he is fully qualified he is so familiar with the old patina and colours of the oxidized wood found in a genuine piece he can recognize the feeble attempt at copying this which is made by the faker.

It is a great pity that this most interesting occupation of restoration and conservation is so abused. Perhaps one long-term answer to this problem is to have more and more experts in the field and so expose the fakers. I can only hope that my writing will serve as one small contribution to this end. It is now in your hands to follow this interesting occupation and enjoy the great challenge it offers. You can become an expert; it's up to you.

Repairing cross-banding on a drawer from a walnut chest

Index

Drawers, restoration of: procedure, techniques, 49-51; repair of locks, 74-5; treatment of runners, 49
Dry rot, 40
Dyeing: to match colour, 79-80; variety, choice of dyes, 82-3

Ebony lining, in marquetry, 66
Embossing of leather table tops, 77-8
Equipment, workshop, 41-4

Fading, in old furniture, reproducing colour of, 81-2, 83
Faking, borderline between restoring and, 92-3
Feather banding (herring bone), restoring, in walnut furniture, 54-5
Feet, restoration of carved, 87
Filling, of chipped areas of paint, 60-1
Finishing techniques: choosing stains, dyes, 81-3; colour matching, 79-80; formula for wax polish, 81; French polishing, 80-1; restoring colour and surface, 83-5
Fluting, restoration of, 87
French polish: application, 80-1, 85; in restoration of lacquer work, 69-70; removal of old, 83-4
Fretwork galleries, brackets, 76
Furniture beetle, 40

Gesso compounds, uses of, 60-1, 63, 69, 89
Gilding methods, 63-4, 69-70, 78
Glass, repair, restoration of, 88-9
Glass-cutters, use of, 88-9
Glue, properties of, 41-2
Glue blocks, 48
Glue pots, 43
Gluing: before treating for woodworm, 48; of metal inlays, 72-3; techniques in restoring marquetry, 66
Gold leaf, application of, 63-4, 69-70, 78
Gold size base, 63-4
Grain, filling in, 51
Grease, removal of, 83
Grinding, of tools, 45-6
Grinding wheel, 43
Grindstones, 45-6

Hammering, of brass inlays, 72
Hammers, choice of, 42
Handscrews (G-cramps), 42
Herring bone banding, restoration of, 54-5
Hinges, in rule joints, 51-2
Honing of tools, 45-6

Hot water treatment: for blistering in veneers, 55; for restoring bruises, 90-1
Humidifiers, 37

Ink stains, removal of, 90
Inlays, metal, restoration of, 72-6; *see also* Lining

Keys, cutting of, 75

Lacquer furniture, restoration procedure, techniques, 68-71
Leather table linings, 77-8
Legs, restoration of carved, 87
Lever locks, 75
Lining: in lacquer furniture, 70; in marquetry, 66; in restoring paintwork, 62
Linseed oil, for stain removal, 90-1
Locks, repair, restoration of, 74-5
Lubrication of metal parts, 73-5

Mahogany: chest of drawers, restoration of, 47-51; colour changes, 39; matching, 48
Marquetry, restoration of, 65-7
Matching: dyeing, staining techniques, 79-80; of colour in painted furniture, 61; of seasoned timber, 48, 50-1, 57; of veneers for marquetry, 65, 66-7
Metal inlays, fittings, restoration of, 72-6
Methylated spirit: for removal of perished varnish, 68, 83-4; use in stain removal, 91
Mortice and tenon joints, repair in oak furniture, 58-9
Mouldings: brass, repair of, 73; crossgrain, in walnut furniture, 53-4; loose repair of, 48; restoration of carved, 87
Mounts, brass, restoration of, 73

Naphtha stains, use of, 82

Oak: colour changes, 39; colour matching, 57; restoration techniques, 56-9
Oil stones, 43, 44, 45-6
Oxalic acid: for removal of ink stains, 90; care in use of, 82; use to recover colour of oak, 57

Paint strippers, for removal of old varnish, 84-5
Painted furniture, restoration of, 60-2
Paintwork, in restoration of lacquer furniture, 69-70
Paperhanger's paste, for relining table tops, 77-8